My Real Life

By Bob Bay

*God Bless You Brad!
I pray you are able to
walk in peace & joy for
all your days!*

Bob

My Real Life
Copyright © 2019 by Bob Bay

ISBN: 978-578-55855-4

Contact information for author:

Bob Bay
Email address: bobbay@reallifeministries-stl.com
Facebook: reallifeministries-stl
Website Address: reallifeministries-stl.com

Scripture quotations are New King James unless otherwise noted and quoted from http://www.biblegateway.com

Contents may not be reproduced in whole or part without the written permission of the author. Contact author directly for permission to use or quote material.

Cover Design: Tonya Brewer

Printed in The United States of America. All rights reserved under International Copyright Law.

My Real Life

By Bob Bay

Introduction

I grew up in a typical working class home. The specific events that happened as I grew up contributed to who I would become but they are not the focus of this book. We all have a story. My story, like most, is not all that different. In a world where we all feel in some way that we are different and nobody really understands what we are going through or how we feel, we are not alone.

My drinking started when I was around fifteen years old by chance hanging out with older kids in my neighborhood. I would occasionally smoke pot but rarely in the beginning because it just made me paranoid. Before it all came crashing down I was drinking every day, smoking weed almost everyday and using some kind of drug like meth, or cocaine on any day I could get it. I did what people who abuse drugs and alcohol do—at times endangering the lives of the people closet to me.

My wife, Pam, is an important part of my story. We met when we were seventeen in a fast food restaurant. I was signed up to leave for the army, not looking for a relationship. Yet, somehow that night I knew that

I would one day marry her. She played "hard to get" until I gave up and moved on, then she came after me. We got married on my nineteenth birthday, she was still eighteen. We were two kids without a clue pretending to be adults.

In our fairytale, I was her prince and she was my princess, each of us looking to the other to fill the loneliness and need inside—something beyond our capabilities. We had a lot of heartaches to walk through ahead.

It is God's grace and mercy that allowed us to stay together through it all. During my lowest points she has been strong, and when she has been down, that's when I was at a point to lift us up. There certainly have been times when we could have given up on each other and didn't. Now here we are almost 35 years later still in love, still lifting each other up, and still growing in our journey.

If you or someone you love is caught in a lifestyle of addiction, you don't need to be reminded of what is involved in it. Whether you are single or with someone and have a family, when you're hurting and feel alone, it's all the same.

This book is about my journey out of all of that. I chose to focus on what was behind my behavior, not on the way it manifested.

I could never have imagined, on that day in 1989 what was going to happen, where we would be now.

And that is where my story begins...

AND THEN I WAS BORN AGAIN

Chapter 1

I felt like I was on a sinking ship. As I sat in the room full of people my world was shrinking and falling in on me. The room felt like it was spinning. So much so, that I was holding onto the table in front of me to keep from falling out of my chair.

The Army chaplain sitting across the table from me hadn't even noticed. I couldn't understand why. I literally felt like I would lose my balance at any moment and fall on the floor.

In the background I could hear the voice of another chaplain talking, I had no idea what he was saying. The room seemed to spin faster and faster, and like that last little soap bubble caught in the whirlpool of the tub drain, I was spinning with it. And, just when I felt I could hold on no longer, the speaker would say the word "God".

I couldn't understand anything before or soon after he said it. That word was like a clap in my ear to bring me back from the edge. This happened three or four times and then the seminar was over and I was walking out the door—numb and in a fog. I felt like I had just woke up from a crazy dream and was still trying to figure out if it was real.

I was an E-5 sergeant in the Army and an acting platoon sergeant; which was a position above my rank and in truth above my current abilities. I was 22 years old, married with an 18-month-old baby. Wonderful opportunities had opened up to me, and I stepped in.

My wife loved me, my daughter was precious, and my young military career was off to an incredible start. There was a problem though, a problem I was in desperate denial about. I also happened to be addicted to methamphetamine and alcohol.

The seminar I was attending was hosted by Army chaplains and its purpose was to give us tools on how to deal with stress. I was told a few days earlier I was to attend. No one had said anything about why I had been chosen. It's possible they told me a standard military reason that I had to attend, but quite honestly I can't remember if they did.

There are few details I remember about that weekend. One I do remember was taking a stress test that measured the level of stress in a person's life. It asked all kinds of questions about situations in your life. Things like do you have financial difficulties and are you in the middle of a divorce? Have you lost a loved one recently? Those are some of the negative questions asked. There were also positive questions, like did you have a new baby or get a promotion at work in the last year? We answered yes or no to the questions and at the end you tallied up your yeses and that gave you your score.

The chaplain explained that stress whether good or bad took a toll on you emotionally and physically. He said if you scored from zero to something like 200 that was acceptable. From 200 to 400 you needed to follow certain guidelines to help ease the stress. From 400 to 600 you really needed to do things to reduce stress because it could create health problems over time. If you had a score of 600 or more you were in imminent danger to your health and psychological well-being. I scored just over 1000.

I didn't need a test to tell me I had too much stress. I had put us in financial ruin with my drug use. At work I was barely able to function because of my need to maintain a web of lies and excuses to cover my behavior. My wife, Pam, was more than ready to leave and take our daughter with her. Sadly, in a way, I wished she would so she would stop reminding me how messed up everything was.

I had hurt, disappointed, taken advantage of and used everyone that I cared about. I blamed them and anyone or anything possible for all of my problems. Not once did it ever play out in my mind that it was my fault.

So there I was walking out of the seminar in a complete fog. What had just happened? I thought I was having a nervous breakdown. Why, when I would be on the edge of screaming out loud, would everything stop and I felt peace when I heard the word God? What was happening?

Some would describe this as my moment when I "hit bottom". The sad reality though is that there is no real "bottom" to the pit you're falling into when you're in the life of addiction. There are only ledges you land on that briefly stop you from falling. From there you begin to climb out or lose your footing and continue to fall. The farther you fall, the farther it is to climb out, unless of course, you die first.

In my situation, God had sent me a lifeline in that moment. I was about to grab on with all I had.

At the same time that all this was going on, a person who was very close to me had checked themselves into a treatment center. He called me and told me he was going to a meeting the next night and asked me if I would come with him.

I had given up on ever being able to make it out of the life I was living. I was settling on surviving for as long as I could. My thoughts were, it wouldn't be long. But, I did believe this person could make it out so, I agreed to go with him for support.

The meeting was held in a treatment facility so of course there were several patients at the meeting. There were also several people from the outside.

As the people shared I began to identify with them, I felt many of the same things. By the end I was crying. I didn't want to, it just happened. These people were telling my story.

I knew what I had to do. I had to quit drinking and doing drugs. The drugs were obviously killing me, but I was going to have to quit drinking too. Drinking was just a slower death sentence. There were so many situations that had caused me trouble where drinking was involved, it was clear that it had to go too.

I remember the last beer I had. It was around 10 am, I was sitting at my kitchen table looking at it. Thoughts ran through my mind about what life would be like without it. I had no idea what my future held but I knew this had to stop.

In the Army there was a program I had heard of called the amnesty program where you could turn yourself in if you had a drug problem without fear of punishment. The main condition being you had to request help before you were caught doing drugs.

A quick lesson was soon to be learned about the difference between punishment and walking in the consequences of your actions.

I asked to meet with my commander and because I was breaking the chain of command he asked the First Sergeant to come in with us. I told them I had ten days leave and I needed that time off because I had a drug problem and I needed to quit. The First Sergeant jumped up and said he'd take my rank. I replied, "with all due respect First Sergeant, you can't do that because of the amnesty program." He was pretty mad but our commander stepped in to diffuse the situation.

I don't know why my commander gave me the time off. Maybe he could tell I was sincere. Maybe he was a believer and God spoke to his heart. I could never ask him. Later during my mandatory drug counseling I was told I should have immediately been taken to the hospital for mandatory supervised detox. My commander would've been responsible for anything that went wrong during those ten days. Looking back I can see that a lot could have gone wrong but God was watching out for us both.

It was a horrible ten days. I slept a lot, felt sorry for myself, treated Pam horribly and went to meetings.

Physically it was terrible, emotionally it was even worse. It felt like I would never be "normal" again.

Prior to all of this Pam and I would go to one of the large lakes we lived near. We had an old aluminum boat we had borrowed from Pam's dad. So, when we needed to get out of the house and have a little fun, this provided an inexpensive way to do so.

A few weeks had past and it was springtime in Texas. We thought we would head out to the lake with some of our neighbors and friends for a cookout. It would be our first trip out since I quit drinking. It seemed like a good way to get away from everything I was going through.

In the past on those trips beer was the focus of my relaxing. The lake was really just a change of scenery. On those trips we had so little money I would often have to choose between gas for the boat, ice and a cooler for my beer or just the beer itself. I usually chose gas and beer and would drink the beer warm. That is where my priorities were.

On this trip there would be no drinking for me. Other people were drinking and some of them smoking weed. It was strange that day, I don't know if there were still effects of detoxing or not but it was like I was in a plastic bubble. People talked and occasionally laughed but what was being said never really registered. It felt like I was watching everything on television and not actually there.

Pam says we had the boat there that day but I don't even remember putting it in the water. Neither of us remembers any specifics of that day, just how weird it felt. We barely interacted with anyone.

These people had been our friends and neighbors for a couple years but the common bond we all had was drinking, smoking weed, doing meth and living in each others dysfunction. Up until then we all seemed so close. I now felt like an outsider. I made them feel uncomfortable and they made me feel the same.

After a short while it clouded up and started to rain. We left and that was the last outing we went on with our "friends". We still had our "Hi how ya doing" moments across the fence or on the street. Things were just not going to be the same.

To be fair, some of them may have been worried I would turn them in. It was often a concern when someone we sold drugs to would disappear and we heard rumors they had been caught. A person could sometimes work a deal for a lighter sentence if they agreed to help get the next person up the ladder. Most of us were in the army so we had to be doubly careful.

Later, one of the guys tried to antagonize me into drinking a beer. "What, are you some kind of bible thumper now, you too good to have a beer with me now?" I tried to be nice in those cases. I wasn't a bible thumper or too good. In fact, I was a wreck and knew it. I also knew that drinking a beer or that guy's approval was not going to help in any way.

I had been trying for almost nine months to stop using meth, rarely making it for more than a few days. When I drank my ability to say no to everything else left and I would be right back at it, each time saying this is the last time.

I knew if I went back to using now there would be

terrible consequences. The army now knew what was going on and was keeping an eye on me. I was also out of chances with Pam. Going back meant Pam leaving and taking my daughter with her.

We had to get out of that environment, things had to change. Just a short time later our landlord came into our trailer while we were gone. He took our kitten and got rid of it. He said we were not allowed to have it but we had paid a pet deposit. This was our opening to break our lease without penalties. We found a little farm house two miles down the road for rent.

We would be moving out of that place that had so many temptations and bad memories. But there was another lesson I had to learn before we moved.

This was my season of decision. This was the time period when I said inside myself, "I don't care what it takes, I never want to drink or do drugs again." I have looked back on this time period more times than I can count. So many things could have gone differently. I know God orchestrated events and situations to work in ways that were going to accomplish in me the things that needed to be done.

From the beginning I knew God was with me, I sensed Him, but I did not understand anything about Him. He would do things that I would just understand that it was Him because there was no other explanation.

I would soon understand that this was my 'born-again" season, and after the drugs and alcohol were gone the problem would be me. I also came to understand over time that I would need to continue to grow and mature for the rest of my life.

There had to be the moment though when I started all over again, understanding only one thing—that I understood nothing about life. I did not know how to be a healthy, happy, productive member of society. I did not know how to be a good husband, father, son, brother, friend, leader, follower—nothing. But, if I was willing, God could and would teach me, parent me, in a way that I could become all those things. Not perfectly, but successfully.

The willingness would be tested so many times over the years. God removed the desire to drink and do drugs but he did not remove the desire to want to take the easy way out when things get hard. He did not remove my want to for things to be instantly different. He did not remove the struggle inside to do the right thing rather than doing the thing that makes me feel good or better or different.

He did give me the ability to feel and experience life in ways I could never have imagined. He gave me a love for my family I can't express in words. He gave me a peace about myself that I never would have thought possible. He gave me so much more than I could have imagined, but He had to prepare me for it all as I grew. I wish I could tell my entire story here but there is too much. These are some of the pieces that fit together to make me who I am today.

Of course this is not the beginning nor is it the end. This is just a good place to start. A good place to start my real life.

"The Router"

Chapter 2

Not long after I had stopped drinking and doing drugs I began to understand that my life pretty much revolved around those two things. It was obvious even to me that I drank every day and that getting high or using something consumed my thoughts. What was not clear to me, even in the least little bit, was how deeply the addictive behavior was ingrained in who I was.

After a month or two of sobriety I was getting to the point where the physical and psychological numbness was gone. The initial detox had subsided, my emotions were not quite as raw but my nerves were on the edge. I thought if I could just find a hobby, something to occupy my time, maybe I wouldn't think about things so much.

One of the things I really loved to do when I was in school was make things in shop class. It seemed like the perfect hobby to fill my time. My challenge was I had no woodworking tools or place to actually build anything so I thought woodcarving may be the way to start. The disaster I'd caused in our finances meant there was only enough money for me to buy a very cheap set of carving knives. After a quick trip to the hobby store my new adventure began.

Like most project ideas I've had in my life, this one started small and manageable but soon evolved into a grandiose endeavor. Skipping several stages of evolution in my story, I soon envisioned building a roll top desk for Pam. I began to drag home every piece of wood, junk furniture or scrap I thought I could use. I still had no real tools though and quickly realized I needed a power tool called a router.

This tool is used to shape edges, cut grooves and so many other things. It would be so useful. There was only one problem. A router and the basic bits to go with it cost the equivalent of a monthly electric bill, and there was no way Pam was going to go for that.

It seems crazy looking back and must have seemed even crazier to someone on the outside; there is no explaining it, but I had to have that router. It was going to allow me to do things that would make me happy. When I felt happy I would not feel the way I normally did. This was my goal and the consequences of the choices made to reach that goal were quickly rationalized away.

I, of course, did not actually process it this way. I did not understand at the time what was happening. I just knew I had to have it, which meant coming up with a plan. Well, there was no plan. I went and bought it and it felt wonderful as I put it in the trunk of my car. I began to think of all the things I could build with it. Then I got home and realized Pam would know I had a new tool and she would start asking questions about how I bought it.

I had learned from my drug days that these things

had to be handled just right when it came to breaking news to Pam that she would not like. However, I never really learned how that worked successfully so I kept the router hidden in the trunk.

A week went by, maybe more, as I quietly thought of how wonderful it was going to be using my new router. The problem remained that I still had to figure out a way to tell Pam I now owned the new router. It was a momentary illusion of bliss that was sure to come to an end.

I wish I could tell you how Pam found out. Knowing who I was then, I'm sure it was at the point when I was absolutely caught in a lie I couldn't lie my way out of. I don't know why I didn't just take it back. There had been at least one time that I used it before being discovered and that may be why I couldn't take it back. Whatever the case was, there was a lesson about to be learned the hard way—which is how I seem to learn best.

This was a turning point in my life. Up until then I thought if I could just stop drinking and doing drugs everything would be okay. I had believed that without the drinking and drugs my relationship with Pam would be fine, my money problems would work out, and my work life would be okay. But none of that was guaranteed.

It was at this time period when I began to realize what they meant when they told me my drinking and drugs were just a symptom of something deeper inside me. My behaviors with the router were exactly the same as those during my drug times. If I did not do something about those issues, nothing in my life would change.

This would prove to be a very difficult task. I had

spent most of my life up to this point subconsciously, and sometimes unconsciously, trying to cover my feelings with something. At the time I had no idea that was what I was doing. I was trying to find a solution to a problem I didn't know I had.

My solution was to replace my addictions with something positive or productive. It seemed like a great idea at the time. No body gets hurt, right?

If only it were that simple...

I learned over the next several years that there were problems with simply trying to replace an addiction with something positive. Don't get me wrong, there are benefits to it, but it is not the solution. Filling my life with positive things did not mean the negative things would automatically fall out the other side. I still had no way to process what was going on inside me in a healthy positive way. It was just masked by "positive" behavior.

It would work for a while then something stressful or hurtful would happen. I would spend money I didn't have on something I didn't need to make me feel better and then end up feeling worse. Or, I would vent in an outburst of anger at people who had done nothing to deserve it.

I still craved approval and acceptance so I often committed to do things for people that I really didn't have time for. Then, when I didn't get the response I expected, I would build resentments inside. Without a way to process it I was a walking time bomb waiting to explode on someone I loved when they least expected it.

Often I would *way* over commit myself to the point

where no one received a full effort for what I promised. With work, time with Pam or my kids, favors for friends or other family members, I would be so stretched they would only get about seventy percent of me. The rest of my time was spent thinking about what I had to do next or worrying about what I didn't get done.

All this behavior made me late to almost everything in my life. No one could count on me to carry through with my commitments. My life was spent on dealing with whatever situation's demands were the loudest or most pressing at the present moment.

A lifetime of shame and feelings of not being "good enough", caused me to overcompensate with perfectionism that made me highly critical of myself and others.

The many bad choices I had made during the time I was using drugs filled me with regret. I lived completely *reacting* to life—not living it. There was no hobby that could take care of that.

The revelation I received from "the router" lesson set my real recovery in motion. At the time, I had no idea the role of people pleasing and approval seeking, combined with low self-worth, shame, regret, and bitterness would have in my life.

Slowly, over time, with my new found revelation that there was so much more to recovery than just staying off drugs and alcohol, I began to see the role and affects of those other things as well. All that came from that initial realization that the same behavior behind the router was the same behavior behind the drugs.

It would take time and a lot of effort to get me beyond myself but I did not have to do it alone. Thank God!

As a side note, I later would go on to become a carpenter and cabinetmaker. I used that router for many years. When I used it God would remind me of what it started as and how far I had come.

One day I was on a job repairing fire damage in an old church, and the maintenance man was watching me routing an edge around a door with a new router I had. We talked for several minutes about everything a router could do and he asked a lot of questions. So, the next day I boxed up that old router and the book I used to learn the many different ways to use it. I gave him the router and book and briefly shared this story. Turns out, he was on a journey of his own. I don't know what has become of him or that router, but I hope it helped him the way it did me.

"THE DREAM"

Chapter 3

A short time after the router lesson I was still struggling with questions about what was happening in my life. I had plenty of time to think about things now that the fog of chemicals and alcohol had been cleared out.

I still blamed a big part of my troubles on everyone around me. I was now walking in the consequences of years of bad choices. As a result, things were pretty bad off. Being the person I was at that time, I felt that what I was doing was *such* a great thing. I had come clean on my drug problem and stopped doing drugs and alcohol. It really seemed to me that people should be more understanding and give me a break.

In my mind I felt that people weren't treating me fairly. It seemed to me that I was doing a really noble thing and I should not be punished for what happened in the past.

My sponsor would often tell me I had spent *years* breaking promises and making excuses. He asked me why I would expect people to see things differently after only a few months.

It was during this time while I was complaining to him, after a meeting we had attended, he seemingly out of the blue asked me if I was kneeling down and praying every day. Not knowing why he asked, I told him I talked to God every day but I didn't have to kneel to do that.

He told me I should kneel and pray every morning and ask God for His help in these things. I quickly explained that I could just talk to God while I lay in bed or sat on the couch. God didn't expect me to kneel down. He explained that we need to learn humility, and one way to learn humility is to kneel when we pray.

I told him I would think about it, while on the inside I was thinking he was crazy. This was often my way of handling things I did not agree with. I would say something to make you think I was open to your idea, all the while thinking you're wrong.

Thinking back on that day, I cannot remember what I did that day once I got home. There is no memory of even thinking about the conversation again or what Pam and I did before going to bed. I just know I went to bed.

Then I had "The Dream."

It is called "The Dream" because even though I have often had vivid dreams this one changed my life. This dream was a point of suddenly understanding something and knowing it was not a random fabrication of my brain. My subconscious wasn't capable of it.

In this dream, as with others I've had, it started with a buildup of random events. I don't remember what they were about. Suddenly, I woke up (still part of the dream) from hearing the pleading screams of a child.

"The Dream"

"Help me, please help me!" After almost 30 years I can still hear it clearly in my head.

"Help me, help me, please help me!" There is no way to describe the panic, terror and helplessness coming from that voice. As I sat up in bed, in my dream, I realized my bed was floating in the air inside of a huge space that seemed like the inside of a volcano. There was fire all around in the walls and smoke. The space seemed as big as four or five football fields around with sharp looking black jagged rock walls rising up. I could see no outside light, just the light of the flames.

But the child's screams for help was not all I heard. There was a deep terrifying roar or growl from some kind of monstrous beast below my floating bed.

The beast seemed as close as the child but I could not see where. The fear I felt, from the sounds the beast made, caused me to forget the child's screams for a moment. This dream felt so real! I just knew if this beast got me, there was no escaping.

Then the child's cry for help pulled me back, catching my attention once more. I realized it was coming from the end of the bed. As I looked I saw two sets of small fingers grasping the edge of the foot board of the bed. It was as if this child was hanging off the end of the bed holding on for dear life. I had no idea of how high we were floating above the bottom of the volcano. I had no idea how close the beast was.

The sickness I felt in my stomach was so real. I was overwhelmed by fear. I could hardly breathe between the smell of rotten egg and terror it was like someone was sitting on my chest.

I couldn't leave the child hanging there, but paralyzing fear of the beast prevented me from moving to help the child. Yet, I had to do something.

"Help me, help me!" The screams continued.

It felt like the child was bait to lure me to the edge so the beast could snatch me and drag me into the fire. Again, I knew I had to do something. Pulling on the sheets of the bed with my hands and pushing with my feet, I dragged myself inch by inch to the foot of the bed. I was almost completely paralyzed by the fear. The closer I got to the foot board the louder the beast wailed and growled and the more the child screamed.

I felt like I was clawing my way through mud and was barely able to move. My throat was so choked down from fear I couldn't even tell the child that I was coming.

Finally, I reached the end and stretched out my arms and put my hands over each of the child's hands in an effort to help them hold on. At the same time, I managed to pull my knees up under me. I could now reach over the end of the bed to grab the child and pull it to safety; but I was so scared to look over the edge.

The screams and growls were constant and my ears were ringing from the noise. I had to do it, I had to reach over. I pulled everything in me together and forced myself to lean over to grab the child.

Time stood still. The noise moved so far into the background it was like I had earplugs in. I was frozen as I looked into the eyes of the child, eight or nine year's old, scared, terrified, pleading but now, without words, just the helpless look of desperation.

I then realized it was me!

The child that had to be saved was me. Just as time had stood still, and the noise died out as I realized who this child was, time then sped forward and the rage and evil of the beast yelled out in my ears. In an instant I knew I could not save this child alone.

I bolted awake from the dream, still feeling like I couldn't breathe, frantically looking in the darkness of my room for the beast that was about to strike, but he wasn't there.

I scrambled out of bed as fast as I could not thinking of waking Pam or even of my daughter as I ran past her room. So many thoughts were flooding my head I couldn't think. I was just reacting, I was still scared. I dropped to my knees in front of a living room chair, bowed my face into the seat and interlocked my fingers together and started saying the Lord's prayer as fast as I could.

Why? Because I knew with everything in me that God was my only chance of saving that scared little boy inside me. I didn't stand a chance on my own. Why the Lord's Prayer? Because I had no idea what to say, but I knew I had to cry out to Him somehow. The meetings I had been attending always ended with repeating the Lord's Prayer together so I had memorized it. I don't know how many times it took to calm me down, but it seemed like a hundred.

There is no doubt in my mind that this dream was an encounter with God. It showed me how helpless I am against things that are clearly out of my control.

Strangely enough, even though in my dream I was alone trying to save myself, and was about to lose before I woke up, I realized the dream was God letting me know He was with me. I was helpless alone, but because He was with me everything would be okay.

My life had gotten to the point where I was completely self-determined and in control of my life, yet completely out of control. Even though I would lie to myself and say the choices I made in life were for my wife and daughter, the truth is, they were for me.

I had locked myself in a prison of hurt and loneliness I created. Then, I got bitter and angry at everyone else for me being there.

I continued to kneel whenever I prayed for some time. Eventually it was okay to just talk to God where ever or when ever I wanted. The humility I needed was not a negative thing; it was an understanding of who I was and how God sees me.

God sees me as that terrified little boy that He will do anything to rescue.

This dream helped me to eventually see that I didn't need to be afraid of God.

I needed to be afraid of being without Him.

Walking The Walk And Trying To Run Away

Chapter 4

The encounter I had with God in that seminar was not my first. He had been working on me for a long time. Looking back, I can see the heartache and misery I could have avoided if I had only stopped running. I was that proverbial frog in the pot slowly being brought to a boil, and I am incredibly thankful I made it out before it was too late. This, of course, would be another lesson I learned the hard way.

Not long after arriving in Texas God would send another lifeboat to rescue me and as it was so many other times, I would not recognize it until much later.

It was early spring in Texas; I was 18 years old and trying to adjust to my new life in the Army. What I imagine many young people experience as they go off to college, I was experiencing in the Army. I was away from home for the first time, living in a dorm style setting with many other young people going through the same things.

This, however, was not my temporary home for the semester. Mom and dad did not drop me off and drive away crying after making sure I was settled in. There were no professors here with homework. There were only formations followed by physical exercise training, then to work as a helicopter mechanic, and then an afternoon formation. These and other things were all being done in preparation for a war or combat situation that may or may not happen during my time of service.

We lived in barracks. Two people to a room, bunk beds, and each person had a wall locker. The wall locker was a cabinet about 4 feet wide and 7 feet tall It had a few drawers, a shelf, and a rod to hang uniforms and some civilian clothes on. That was the extent of our personal space.

The barracks, rooms, and wall lockers were subject to inspection at any time. Everything was expected to be neat and clean. Being in an aviation company I think we had it easier than many other military occupations but for me this was still very hard.

I had always been a "clutter" person. Growing up my room was always piled with clothes and projects with various items at some stage of disassemble. My life was cluttered as well. My mind was always full of half thoughts and ideas. It was filled with expectations for the future with no solid plan for achieving them. I was rarely, if ever, early for anything—usually a few minutes late.

In a military world of *attention to detail* and *being on time*, I struggled. It was difficult being new in that environment. Being away from home and away from my girlfriend was hard as well.

I found myself back in a cycle of coping through the week and drinking heavily through the weekend. There had also been midweek binges that became more frequent. There were connections being made but I would not say that I had friends. Most of the time was spent alone but usually surrounded by people. I am by no means an introvert; I just didn't want people that close to me.

One day I went to the mini PX. This was kind of a convenience store I could walk to. As I left the store with a few snack items a young man approached me and asked me if I attended church somewhere? I said no, and he asked me if I would want to go with him to a midweek service at his church. We talked about a few things, I can't remember what but after a few minutes I agreed to go and I gave him my address so he could pick me up.

To this day I can't say what it was specifically that would have caused me to agree to this. I was generally a loner unless it served a purpose to get me something. I can only attribute it to God's plan for down the road.

The day we had agreed on rolled around and the man came and picked me up. I wish I could remember his name. Anyway, we went to the church but it wasn't in a church. It was a rented space of some kind. There was about 50 people there I guess, maybe a few more. It seemed crowded but I think it was a small room. The group seemed to be a pretty diverse blend of people, much like typical army groups are.

My church background was in a conservative Southern Baptist Church so I was very surprised at the way the service was going. I would best describe it as a charismatic church with a Pentecostal lean. I can't remember anything that was taught during the message, what songs were sung or how long any of it lasted.

There's one thing I do know, something happened during that service and God touched my heart. So much so that I was kind of choked up at the end, and when another man came and asked me what I thought I told him "I think I found what I've been looking for all my life".

I have very little memory of what went on that night but I still to this day remember saying those words—they just came out. I honestly can say I didn't even know I was looking for anything

It was real. When I think back to that moment, it was real. There was not a lot of hype or emotionalism, it was simple. Deep inside I realized there was something missing in my life and God was the answer. They took me home, we talked and I agreed that I should come back for the weekend service.

This would be a great way to end this story—with "And I found Jesus and lived happily ever after". But that is not what happened. There was something else at work in me. Call it what you will but by the weekend I was sure I would not be going back there.

I have tried to remember so many times over the years if there was something in particular that made me feel like I did, but I cannot pinpoint anything. Yes, I was scared of what it would mean to be a church person. Yes, I had mentioned that I had gone to church that night to some people and they were negative and yes, I was drinking a lot by the weekend.

There were lots of things that probably factored into why I felt the way I did, but it is what I did that is important.

I was alone in my room when the man came to pick me up for the Saturday service. I had been drinking and I didn't know what time it was. The man at the door, whom I'll call Tom, was not the first man who originally invited me to church. It was the man I told "I have found what I was looking for all my life".

At the first meeting we talked and I had told him how I felt, I had tears in my eyes, I was vulnerable and it was as if I was a brother to the world. Everything seemed right and hopeful. Now, as I opened the door after his knock, everything was different. I had one goal in mind. Run this guy off and do it in a way that will keep him from ever coming back. I was combative, rude and belligerent; he was calm, confident and consistent. This made me even that more determined. It was horrible. If the roles were reversed I probably would have punched me in the face. He left and did not come back.

I forgot about Tom for the most part. Occasionally I would have a flash memory of the church service or his face, but I had moved on.

I got married and had a new baby. My military career was going great and I was being promoted up the ranks faster than my peers, which brought a whole new set of problems. My drinking had intensified and I began smoking weed and doing other drugs as well.

A lot of things happened in the almost two years after that meeting. Some of them great, but overall my life was on the verge of collapse. I just didn't know it.

Looking back it's easy to see the progression but when I was in the middle of it I had no clue. I had become an alcoholic and drug addict but I just thought I loved to party. I was miserable inside but stayed numb to my feelings by using anything that came my way.

Then one day we received word that there was a new sergeant coming to our company. He was being transferred from another company across base at the other air field. This was incredibly rare for this to happen.

I was a crew chief on a helicopter in a small flight platoon. In my company there were two flight platoons and there was a slight rivalry between the two. I think the competition over who had the best ratings or flew the most missions gave us incentive to work harder. This new sergeant would be taking over the other flight platoon so we had been giving the guys a hard time about what their new boss would be like.

I walked in that morning to see the new guy and there he was. It was Tom!

How could this be? Of the tens of thousands of soldiers stationed there, with only maybe a couple hundred who did our job, and of those few, that he had the necessary rank needed to take over that platoon. Add that to a chance meeting, we had almost two years earlier, at that little church with 50 people, and there is no way this was another "just by chance" occurrence. I couldn't believe it!

I, of course, pretended that we had never met.

Instantly I decided I did not like him and I would make comments about him to my coworkers. But soon I began to notice that the people under him really respected him.

As time went by I was made acting platoon

sergeant of my platoon and our jobs caused us to work more closely together. I soon saw that he did everything by the book. In my case, I believed that the book was something you had to work around and overcome. Rules and regulations seemed to only complicate my life and I looked for the easiest way possible to get the job done.

There were times when our differences would cause strife. This was always on my part, although I did not see it that way at the time. He out-ranked me by two grades so I couldn't do much, but I would be as combative as I possibly could and get away with it.

He, on the other hand, was always projecting professionalism. *I did not understand him.* He did not complain when things were obviously chaotic. In the military decisions from above often make no sense and seem out of touch at lower levels, but he would follow directions and expected others to do the same.

We would run in formation for physical training and a leader would call cadence. That is the song or rhyme called out to keep everyone in rhythm and in step. If you see movies with military formations running or marching you often hear the leader say a line then the group repeats it or has a set reply. Many times there are negative or crude messages or phrases in the songs. He would change the line or words when he led them or when he would be in formation he would skip the cuss words that were said by others.

I watched him for the next year to year and a half walk out his faith. He was open about his beliefs but never preachy. I always saw integrity, honesty and excellence. Everyone respected him but he was never proud or boastful. I don't know how he felt on the inside but he seemed to have a quiet confidence that most people don't have.

Why am I telling you this? Without preaching to me he showed me Jesus. He earned my respect without asking for it. He walked in integrity through situations that most people, including me, would take the easy road to avoid.

I was 22 years old by then. The army promoted me to sergeant well ahead of my peers into a leadership position meant for two grade ranks above mine. I was a prideful, spiteful person. Other sergeants a grade rank above me felt they deserved the job and they would often criticize me. Whenever the opportunity presented itself to rub it in their faces, I would. I made sure I did it in a way that would not allow for any repercussions. Sadly, I also took advantage of the men under me to get ahead. I would often blame them for the things I had fallen short on.

I had earned what I had through very hard work, but once there, because of everything going on in my life, I abused the position entrusted to me in order to protect what I had.

Tom was there when I hit bottom and lost my position and flight status. While others would tease me and make comments about me, he always treated me with respect.

No one else knew about that time of vulnerability three and half years earlier. They did not see the tears or hear my statement of being lost. I never told anyone. But he knew, and never brought it up. Neither did he ever take the opportunity to confront me about my horrible behavior that day he came to pick me up.

He, more than any of my coworkers or fellow soldiers, could have said I told you so. But he did not.

After many months of being off drugs and alcohol I worked up the nerve to ask him if he remembered me because he never let on like he did. He calmly said yes, I remember. All I could say was, I'm sorry.

I have told this story many times over the last 20 plus years. It has been over 30 years since that young man stopped me out in that parking lot to invite me to church.

Had I surrendered my life then I would not be telling this story. God only knows what heartache I would have avoided. The pain I caused to those around me would've been spared. But God knew I would eventually come to Him and He never gave up on me.

That man who walked the walk may never know the impact he has had on my life. Seeing him hold to his beliefs day in and day out in an environment that was not always godly and often very negative was life-changing to me.

I cannot count how many times I've been around young people who were at a decision point in their lives and I've used Tom's example as strength for myself. Knowing that while I may not be responsible directly for a change in their life, the example I set, the walk I walk, could have a huge impact on them down the road.

There have also been people in my life that talk a lot about being a Christian. They talk a lot about Jesus and spout words and slogans about righteousness and values and what God will do for you. But their behavior in the long run did not match their words, and they have had an impact on my life as well. They are small people with big mouths and even though they may get a lot of attention they will never impact people for good the way that man did. I never want to be that person.

There have been times when I've looked for Tom. I've ask old friends if they know where he ended up. It doesn't seem right to tell you his real name but he knows who he is. If it works out one day for me to have the chance to thank him I would like that, but that is not up to me.

The important thing here is that we never know the impact we have on people or where they may be in their journey towards Christ. We can help them or hurt them by the walk we walk more than the talk we talk. I always want to be a walker, not just a talker.

BEHIND THE BARN

Chapter 5

A few months after I had gotten clean I received orders to go to Korea. This was a hardship tour, which meant that my family could not go with me. The tour would last twelve months and at that point I did not have enough time remaining in service to complete the tour. I would either have to re-enlist for another three years or sign a bar to reenlistment. This would cancel the orders but meant I could not change my mind and re-enlist when my time was up.

It was not a hard choice for me at this point. My flight status was lost and it was tough to even find a test flight I could unofficially ride along with for "training" purposes. Between my time in Central America and later in Panama I had spent all the time away from Pam I could handle at this point. With all that had happened with my drug usage, being promoted to the next rank would have been an extreme challenge. My military career was unofficially ended the day I walked into my commander's office. It was officially over ten months later.

I had grown so much during that time. I made all new friends and went to meetings a lot. My relationship with Pam had faced several near ending moments, but we were rebuilding by that point. I was excited at the idea of starting over and the possibilities that lay ahead.

Things rarely end up the way I think they will. But that's not necessarily a bad thing.

Growing up I had two things I thought would be great to do as a job. One was flying, and I had set out to do that in the Army. Originally I had intended to start as a crew chief on a helicopter then transition to pilot. I loved riding around in the helicopter but after seeing what the pilots went through to be up front, I decided I was happy to just ride in back. I loved the feeling of the wind blowing through the helicopter with the doors open and the rush of adrenalin as we banked tight over the trees, up and down over hills and valleys. I have so many great memories of this.

The other thing was building stuff. Shop classes were what got me out of bed in high school. I loved the process of making things.

While attending meetings for recovery during my remaining time in the Army I met a couple that owned a roofing company. There had been several storms go through our area so they needed help. At first I was helping to tear off shingles making an hourly wage. I would work with them in the evenings and on weekends when I could. It was a two-fold plan; partly to make money to get us out of debt and partly to stay busy and keep me out of trouble.

I quickly learned that "tear offs" were no fun, but the guys who laid shingles got paid by the amount of shingles they installed. The owner of the company said hand nailing the shingles was far better than gun nailing them so I learned to swing a hammer. It was incredibly hard roofing in Texas in the summer but I loved it. There was also some light carpentry work and I fell in love with what would later become my new profession.

In the Army I had four years experience as a helicopter crew chief and mechanic but in civilian life this experience did not cross over to a real job.

I had no real documentation of my qualifications so a career in aviation would mean starting at ground level and taking any job I could find and going back to school. It would take years to get to the point where I could do anything other than factory aviation work. The money was not very good at that level either. So, as I considered all this I figured it would be a good time to change careers.

I took some leave time ahead of my separation from the military so we could come back to St. Louis to find a job. I knew nothing of trends in the housing market or the effects of the economy on the building trades. I naively assumed I could just come home and find a job in a couple of days and go back to Texas to finish my time and the job would be there when I got back.

So, in early spring we packed up and left Texas and Army life to come back to Missouri and a job with a small remodeling company.

It did not take long for me to discover that my hopes and dreams were not that important to other people and things were not going to go as planned.

My military life was much different than my civilian life. In the Army there was little concern for profitability. I was trained and later trained others to do their jobs and task in specified ways. If someone took a lot longer to train, you invested the time into them to get it right. Their lives, and in turn your life, might one day depend on that soldier doing their job quickly and effectively.

In the Army your ability to train leaders reflected on you well, and you would be rewarded for it in the future. In this new civilian life people often saw you as a threat to their job if it looked like you had potential to out perform them, so they had an incentive to see you fail. I'm sure that not all civilian work is that way, or that all military units are that way, it seems to be the normal...

I left the Army in March 1990, by that fall I found myself working in a cabinet factory out in a little town an hour and a half outside St. Louis and living on a 280 acre farm as caretaker in exchange for rent.

The time with the remodeling company was a nightmare and there didn't seem to be many other employment opportunities where I was, so when my father-in-law suggested I look for work in his little town I did, and I found the cabinet job. We also found the farm and caretaker job through my father-in-law. I had never worked so hard in my life. I worked 60 hours a week building cabinets and then went home to take care of the farm—it was tough.

That winter we had bad ice storms. This meant I had to keep the cows in the upper field where I could keep an eye on them. Some of the neighboring farms had cows fall through the ice on their ponds and die.

Another farmer had cows slip and fall on the ice and break their legs. We didn't lose any but it meant feeding and watering them in the barn lot which resulted in a large amount of extra work and time.

The farm house was entirely heated by a wood furnace. When we moved there in October there was no wood cut. The property owner did however, have a large supply of logs that he was going to saw up for fence posts that he let me cut into firewood . As you can imagine that still meant several hours a week cutting and splitting firewood to stay warm. Despite all the very hard work, Pam and I still look back on that time of our lives as being very happy.

Work at the cabinet factory was going well and I was put in a position I really enjoyed—designing new layouts for drilling cabinet pieces to make assembly easier and faster.

That December our first daughter turned three and Pam was pregnant with our second child. I remember all of us piling on the four wheeled ATV to go out to the woods to find a Christmas tree. There were several inches of snow on the ground and we ran out of gas a half mile from the house. I hoisted my 3 year old up on my shoulders, grabbed the base of the tree in one hand and we headed off through the snow to the house. It was beautiful.

It was so peaceful out on the farm. At night you could only see one light from the porch of our closest neighbor, about a half mile away. We were mostly surrounded by woods and cattle farms.

We still had our share of problems. Money was

incredibly tight. There were conflicts with coworkers at times and being a city boy, taking care of cows and all the things that I had to learn about them was a challenge.

At night, after I would finish my chores and make sure the cows were good, I would sometimes go out behind the barn. From there our neighbor's light was blocked. The ground sloped gradually away to a 40 acre pasture and then a creek separated it from the woods.

There were no sounds of civilization here. On really clear nights, way off in the distance, you could sometimes see the blink of an antenna beacon. This was my church, my sanctuary, where I met with God. Pam and I had tried to go to a church in town but it wasn't right, so it was behind the barn where God would meet me in the quiet.

It was there behind the barn, where I ended up one night in January. There was no moonlight shining over the pasture that night, a light sleet was gently falling making a static sound on the roof of the barn, and I was there to talk to God.

Pam and I often read the bible together, taking turns reading stories from the white King James Bible given to her by her grandparents when she was young. At that stage of my walk it was very hard to connect the stories I read with my real life.

I usually just stood and thought of Him, sometimes talking out loud about questions I had. I didn't know at that time that the peace I felt behind the barn was God's peaceful presence.

That day was different. I was struggling with a

decision and either choice left me scared of what might happen. I had received a notice several weeks earlier that I was being called back into service for Desert Storm. Under the rules of my contract when I first signed up for the Army, I was on inactive reserves for three years after leaving active duty.

This meant that in times of crisis I could be reactivated back into full-time service. When I had left the Army, almost a year earlier, the idea that I would be recalled never even occurred to me.

I don't really remember the moment we found out. Pam says my parents had called and told her I had an official looking letter from the government. I used their address as my forwarding address on my separation papers. I told them to open it and they read it to us.

I remember having the conversation with my boss about being recalled. He had a very somber tone to his voice. It made it seem more real the way he offered his condolence, as if he might know something I didn't.

There was a number on the letter I received that I could call if I had questions. I was able to get information about what my options were. One option was to file for an exemption. One reason I could use that had a double exemption was that we were caretakers on a farm and my wife was pregnant. Since she was pregnant she wouldn't be able to take care of the farm by herself. Another was that I was in a critical position in my work and it would hinder their ability to continue if I left.

I sent them paperwork to request exemption but received no reply. As the days and weeks passed, and my time to report came closer, I had to make a decision.

Would I ignore the report date and hope for an eventual exemption or would I prepare to leave and report as instructed unless I heard otherwise?

Leaving meant losing the farm. My orders said I could be gone for as long as a year. Since Pam was about to have our second baby there was no way she could stay on the farm by herself.

Leaving also meant I would lose my position at work. Someone would have to fill my position, and after a year of being gone I would probably be put back into production.

Those were the immediate problems we faced, but even at 23 years old I understood that there was the ultimate possibility I would not come back. I was being reactivated to go to war. When you're that age you don't think it will happen to you but the idea was there. I thought about my little girl and the new baby on the way and the possibility I would never see him or her. Pam and I had been through so much in our young lives and it seemed as though we were finally working things out and now this.

So there I was, behind the barn, with the decision needing to be made and feeling overwhelmed by it all. As I thought about it all and talked out loud about how I felt it just seemed too big to deal with. I could make the wrong decision and ruin everything.

And then suddenly, I knew what I had to do. I would honor my commitment to the Army and God would take care of everything.

At this point and time in my life, I had experienced

several times when I knew God had made Himself known to me. There were no other explanations for those times that made sense. This was different, in that it wasn't just a feeling of His peace being *inside* me. It wasn't just the reassuring peace that *came over* me. It was as if God had *spoken* to me inside and told me everything would be okay, he would take care of everything.

All I can say about it is that at that moment, I knew that I knew, that God had just talked to me and everything would be okay. It was not an audible voice. There was no burning bush. But, I knew it wasn't just me thinking it.

It took several years before I would openly talk about that night with people. I was afraid they would think I was crazy for thinking God would talk to me.

Pam and I discussed my decision and it was done. We would pack up our belongings to be stored while I was gone and Pam and Cassie would move back to St. Louis and stay with my parents.

I can't remember what day it was when the movers came to pack our things; just that it was warmer than it had been in a while. The sun was shining and things were thawing out from the hard icy winter. Several of the cows had new calves. It was March in Missouri so spring was close but it can still be cold and sometimes snow, but not on that day.

We had worked so hard to get the farmhouse ready to move In and make it our home. All the countless hours taking care of the cows, checking fences, splitting firewood, had now come to an end. I was sad.

We only kept what Pam would need for day-to-day life with Cassie. I had a couple changes of clothes and everything else was packed up and would be stored somewhere at the government's expense for the next year until I returned.

Pam, Cassie and I moved to St. Louis and then I went on to Alabama to receive my refresher training and wait for orders to see where I would be sent.

My time in Alabama was filled with boredom and missing my family. There were guys there that came before us that were receiving orders to go all over Europe and the Middle East. The days would start with morning formation, each of us eagerly waiting for new information. Nothing new would come and we would be released until the afternoon formation where we would wait again.

Once our initial refresher training was done there were very few things to do between formations. Several of us would go bowling in the mornings and then watch news footage of what was happening with the fighting in the afternoon. Nighttime was hard. I would think of Pam and Cassie, the farm and sometimes what my future might hold. The last time I had lived in army barracks my downtime would be filled with drinking and loud music. It was strange to be in that environment and not drink.

I met a couple of guys that were Christians and we would talk about who God was. I knew Jesus had died to save me and I knew God loved me but beyond that I knew very little. My idea of who God is, was different than most of their ideas. One of the guys though, took the time to explain things from the Bible in ways I could relate to. He was sincere in his faith and it was real to him, it was encouraging.

This all went on for weeks, the news was reporting on how quickly we had pushed Saddam's forces back and that we had met little resistance. Then it was over, we were told we had one day to out process and we would be on planes home the next day.

It was chaos filing through stations, filling out paperwork. I couldn't believe how fast they wanted us out. The Army never seemed to want you to hurry like this unless it was to do something you did not want to. Then it became clear. One of the guys in the group said they wanted us out so fast because if we were active more than 30 days we would be eligible for a lot more benefits. It had been 27 days; we would be out at 28 days. I would soon find out what this meant but at that time I was just happy to be going home.

What would I do now? The farm position was the only way we could make it with me working at the cabinet factory and now it was no longer an option. My family and I were back in St. Louis, there was no way I could commute. When I applied for unemployment it was denied. The cabinet factory said they had an opening for me but I couldn't drive the hour and a half each way to get there for the money they paid. To make matters worse my insurance with the cabinet company was lost.

It turns out that if I had been in for 30 days the Army would have covered our insurance for Pam to have our baby.

There we were. We had lost the farm, our home. I lost my job by default. Because the Army had gotten me

49

out in less than 30 days I was ineligible for unemployment and we had no insurance. Pam would be having the baby at any time and we had to stay in my parent's basement. I did not understand how this could be happening. When I had been released from service it was clear that God was taking care of things and everything looked like it would be okay. Now everything seemed messed up and I was wondering if God really was in all of this.

Pam had our baby shortly after I came home. There were a lot of things to stress about but our second daughter filled our lives with joy.

I was trying to find my place in the world during this time. Still in my early twenties with a young family to support, things were difficult and my career choices were limited. There was always the option of factory work but my time at the cabinet factory caused me to rethink that. Carpentry work was not readily available at that time so I was bouncing around trying different sales work in hopes of finding something I enjoyed.

The challenge I had was the immediate need to get us a place of our own while at the same time building an opportunity for the future. My plans had once been to go back to school after the Army, but that would have to wait a while longer. The medical bills were coming in from all the people involved with having our baby. It was overwhelming; we owed so much money to so many people. Doctors, the hospital, anesthesiologists, pediatricians and on top of that was the pressure of getting our own place to live.

How is this all going to be okay? I was getting very resentful about everything. I questioned whether I had ever heard from God and if so, why had He abandoned us? It felt as though we had been cheated for following through with my commitment. It was as though we were being punished for serving our country.

When it all seemed too much and felt as if God was not listening, I went to a man I knew who was very smart in business dealings. I explained where I was at and described our financial situation.

He told me I needed to sit down and write a letter to each of the people I owed money to and briefly explain how I was reactivated, that we lost everything and that I was trying to get on my feet again. Let them know I wanted to pay them but it would take time and ask them to please be patient and work with me. That was all I could do.

It wasn't long and we began receiving letters in reply to ours. Over and over they thanked me for my service, wished us well and wrote off the debt. I was astonished. The kindness of these people was amazing. Soon I began to realize that God really was taking care of us. He never said it would be easy or that it would be the way I wanted. He just said everything would be okay.

As weeks and months and years went by I began to see what God's unfolding plan was, and that He had a purpose for all of it.

I needed time out there on that farm working so hard and having that peaceful environment so I would take time to spend with Him out behind the barn. He knew what was coming and that I would need Him to make it through.

Through those situations He would teach me to have faith and trust Him. Even more important than Him orchestrating events to take care of my medical debt's was the lifetime reward of knowing he was there all along. He could have worked it out smooth from the beginning but then I never would have learned what I did, and I would not have the relationship with Him that I do.

The other huge part of this all was that I was perfectly happy to stay on the farm and would have stayed in the little town if this had not happened. But God's plan for us was in St. Louis, not that small town.

My faith and relationship with God at that time was not to the point where He could speak and I would follow. I had to have outside influences pushing me in the right direction. Those influences got me off the farm and back to St. Louis where a lifetime of healing would be able to continue. There were people God would use in different ministries and churches to grow us into the people we needed to be. He even had a plan for my future career and business that would not have been able to happen on the farm.

I would never have guessed that 25 years later I would feel the way I feel about that night out behind the barn. It seemed as if all our dreams were being taken away during that first year after leaving the farm. There were many times I regretted in my heart not fighting the activation and just staying there.

But that's the way life goes sometimes when we follow Him. We don't see the big picture and focus on the immediate troubles we're in, only to later wonder why we ever doubted because it seems obvious that He is with us. You never know what one small act of obedience can mean for the rest of your life.

Pam and I drove out to that farm about 15 years after we left. The gate was open so we drove back to the house. It looked like no one had lived there for years. Weeds and brush had grown up as high as the roof around the house. It made me a little sad to see it that way because of the picture I had in my memory when we left.

We went back by there a couple of years ago. The gate was closed we couldn't drive to the house, but it was clear that people were living there now. The name on the mailbox was the same family name as the owners when we lived there so I guess they were finally able to move back from Colorado.

Maybe one day I'll go back and see if I could spend a minute behind the barn for old time's sake.

Bob's Box Of Stuff

Chapter 6

I have often heard the metaphor that recovery is like peeling an onion. You keep peeling back the layers till you get to the good ones. My challenge was—the deeper I went, the worse things got.

Pam and I had been surrounded by such dysfunction for so long it seemed as though it was normal. Our ways of coping and dealing with situations had developed into who we were on the inside. Every new situation or event in our lives were then filtered through those perspectives and coping mechanisms.

While I was in Texas I had immersed myself in recovery meetings. I had people that could speak into my life but those people were still walking in their own dysfunctions. While they were invaluable in helping me get free of drugs and alcohol and helped me look at some of my relationship issues with Pam, they couldn't take me any farther than they had been. That is meant as no slight to them. It's just that my circle of influence was young in their recovery.

Once Pam and I moved back to Missouri I tried very hard to find a recovery group that I could connect to. I knew that I needed to surround myself with people that were moving in the same direction I wanted to go. There were tools I had been given through those meetings that had helped me to begin to develop better relationships with people and God but I was still very new to using them when we moved.

The program I was part of in Texas was not nearly as wide spread in Missouri. There were times when I would find a meeting and go and there would be no one there. One time I went and there was one person there, a young lady about my same age. I got there a minute or two after the set start time. She asked if I was in a good or bad place because this was the fourth week that no one had showed up but her and she was getting ready to leave. There would no longer be a meeting there.

I tried changing to another similar type meeting but found them to be too narrow in their focus. I wasn't allowed to freely share what was going on in my life and the relationship I was trying to build with God. I felt a little lost in all of it.

In the meetings in Texas I had found a family but they were now very far from me. I had finally gotten to the place where I was willing to go to church but the people there often backed off when I would share my story. The ones that did understand where I came from would many times be critical of the tools God had given me to help me in my recovery.

A few years passed, Pam and I wandered about, trying to find help and healing through many different paths. We were desperately hurting. God had brought me out of so many things, He had done so much inside us but we still were struggling to even be able to function in our daily lives. God used preachers on a local radio station to speak to me things about Him from the bible that I could not understand on my own. We had even started going to a large church in our area.

That church, however, was so big it made it difficult if not impossible for us to connect with the leadership. We got involved in a small group to build connections that were much more personal. The challenge though was that many of the small group leaders were often as dysfunctional as we were so finding guidance and mentoring in those situations was very hard.

There was one woman though, who had a small ministry that attended our church that dealt directly with broken and hurting people. Once a week she had a meeting in her basement and there would be anywhere from 20 to 30 people come from various places. She had walked through many of the same things Pam and I had so when she spoke from her experience and taught things from the Bible it really connected.

As crazy as it sounds, while we were part of that big church we even became small group leaders. For a short while we met a few times in our house. Looking back it was all so messed up, but it was what I needed to create change in my heart.

In a way, we were actually being discipled or mentored in those basement meetings. God was revealing to us who He really was. It wasn't long before the small group of people who were not getting their needs met in the big church decided we should break away and start another church.

It was during this time that bits of my past would come back to trouble me. Up to this point, I mainly focused on staying clean from drugs and drinking and just managing the day to day life. Keeping a job, raising kids, and being a husband was almost more than I could handle. Being in the military combined with recovering from addiction created a lot of instability and geographical change brought on by both had become our way of dealing with life.

A pattern had developed whereby we would just get settled down in a new home and something would happen to force us to move. There were times where a near eviction was involved. Other times, it presented new opportunities filling us with hope and promise that soon fell flat when our old lives caught up with us.

An example of such a move was the time we moved from an apartment that we had to leave because we were behind on rent and they would not allow us to renew our lease. This move was one of those times of opportunity with hope and promise. We were able to move into a house. Now, this house was not a nice house by any means, but it was a refuge for me. It was a miracle the way we got into this house considering circumstances of why we had to leave the apartment.

I really don't know why this move and time was so different. Maybe I had grown enough that I was ready for a deeper more lasting change. Maybe I was just hurting bad enough by this point that I was ready to do whatever it took.

As part of the routine of moving we would box everything up, move and then unpack most of our things.

Some of the boxes would not get unpacked and became known as "keep it stuff" boxes.

"Keep it" boxes contained mementos and memory boxes, most of which had no value other than the emotions connected to each item inside. Each family member had a box. Their name would be written on it with a date noting the last time it was gone through.

As time passed and moves occurred the contents of these boxes would be moved to a larger box. Usually, the only time they were ever opened was during the moving process. On one particular move Pam labeled my box "Bob's s**t". As I said, we were young and early in recovery so this seemed normal. From now on I'll call it Bob's Stuff box.

At this house, the Bob's Stuff box got put on the floor in the basement instead of on a shelf. Somehow the sewer backed up into the basement and got to my box. There were things in the basement that I immediately got out to save once the back up was cleared. Most of the stuff obviously had to be gotten rid of. But I sat my box of stuff aside to dry. Water had only gotten a few inches up on the box. I figured most of the contents had probably not even gotten wet.

As time passed I was so torn at what to do. The items in the box were things like my Army medals, my first clean-time key tag and other similar commendations or mile marker items. There were also things from the past, items connected to the old days that had not been taken out of the box even after I left those times behind. Now I was faced with choices. I didn't want to throw out everything. But some things were not worth keeping. I was afraid to even open the box because of what I might find.

Finally, after a few days I got up the courage to go through the box.

In the past when I would open the box to add to it I would look at some of the things and think about the memories connected to them in a fond way. Sometimes Pam and I would be opening our boxes at the same time. We would hold different items up and ask each other, "Do you remember this?" It was usually fun, even with the things from our past.

This time however, it seemed totally different. Looking back it's still hard to say if the reason I felt different was because the other things going on in my life caused me to view things differently or if it was that as I pulled things out of the box I now had to decide if I should keep it or throw it away. Maybe it was a combination of the two. Irregardless, the feelings were very different that time as I decided what was worth going through the cleaning process and what was beyond saving.

As each item came out I processed the memories connected to it. Some things were very hard to let go of—but they were ruined. Some things were fine and I could have kept them, but as I thought about them the memories were not worth even transferring to a new box. There were things in the bottom of the box that had not come out in many years. I often wondered how they even got in there.

I know there are a lot of people that probably cannot relate to what was happening during this process, but to me it was very intense.

Weeks and months passed after this without me thinking about the box. The rest of my life seemed as though it was falling apart. Work was not going well and we were behind on the rent again. Things between Pam and I were very strained. I had felt very close to God for a while, but now He seemed a thousand miles away. I was beginning to feel hopeless again. The mistakes and negative things of my past kept resurfacing and would deflate me.

I would go back to the tools I had learned in my early recovery and use them to work through each problem now occurring in my life. There were common feelings connected to everything, shame and regret. I couldn't shake them.

Early in my recovery I had gone through the process of admitting the secret thoughts and events of my life and I had experienced a tremendous freedom through that. I had not, however, admitted everything. There were two things that I held on to that I felt I could never share with another human being.

I walked through life feeling like everyone knew about my secrets. Like I had a cartoon bubble over my head that described how awful I was. At the time I did not understand that I was filtering everything in my life through the guilt and shame of those secrets. I did not consciously think that, it just happened.

God began to show me situations in my life and bring up events of my past that were all connected by those same feelings of guilt and shame. Those feelings caused me to want to hide those things even deeper. I would build walls to keep people out without even realizing it. I was again feeling very lonely even when surrounded by people.

All the stuff inside me was slowly cutting me off from God and the people I cared about. I would have temporary relief at times but nothing lasting. And the common ties to all of it were the secrets that I held inside.

It was the "Bob's Stuff" box inside me that needed to be gone through and cleaned out. It was time to finally face the things inside me so they could no longer hold me captive.

As soon as I put it all together, what was going on inside and how it affected me and how it all related to the box event I knew I had to finally talk with someone about these two final secrets in my life. I also knew I had to do it right away or I would lose my nerve.

Please let me give you a word of warning. I do not recommend doing this without very wise council on the matter. Opening up the wrong way at the wrong time with the wrong person could be devastating.

Having said that, I know that if I had been thorough back in the beginning I could have avoided years of heart ache.

I got with my Pastor at the time as quick as I could and shared what was going on in my life. I shared what I felt had been holding me back and I shared my final two secrets. She walked me through each thing and God used her to give me biblical wisdom and understanding.

The weight of the world was lifted off my shoulders. I instantly felt relief. I felt the presence Of God in me. I know He was there already but I could actually feel

Him in a new way. Words really can't do justice to what happened.

Over the years God has used that experience to teach me so much about myself. It taught me how the effects of my past play on the present and the way it shapes my future. Later I would learn, in the Bible from the book of James, that we need to confess our sins to each other so that we can be healed. I also learned that denying hurts or hiding things that have hurt us can cause them to become infected and fester like a physical wound.

I had learned growing up, before "the box" incident, that there was nothing you could do about the past. What's happened, happened, and you just have to move on. The proverbial "time heals all wounds" is simply not true.

There are powerful emotions connected to the memories of events that happened in our past. Once filed in our brain those memories and events can't be erased or deleted no matter how much we try to push them down or block them out. They must be taken out, processed, cleaned off and dealt with.

I have memories that were connected to really hard periods of my life that when I would remember them, the joy or goodness that should have been felt was clouded by the times they occurred in. Once they were taken out and cleaned off I can now look back without regret overshadowing them.

Some of my memories have been filed under new categories. Like many of the stories in this book they serve as valuable lessons rather than painful memories.

The pain of the moment was replaced with wisdom of the experience.

Some of the events of my past were looked at, processed and then thrown out. Just like those items from the box, I can remember them but they no longer are part of me, they are not in my "box", I just remember them being there. And just like the things that were in the box, even if I try real hard I can't remember everything that was in there unless something specific happens that brings it to mind. But I am not remembering the moment the event happened as though I am reliving it; I am remembering the event as an item I pick up, look at and put back down.

When I need to I can use those memories to help me be empathetic to others. I can also remember them to remind me of where I came from and what would happen if I decided to make those same choices again.

An illustration of this are some beer bottle caps I had in the box. They were from different beers I had drank during my time in Central America. I threw the caps out when I cleaned out the box because I don't want to be needlessly reminded of the events connected to those caps.

If the actual caps were left in the box every time I went through the box I would see them and remember having them. I have seen a lot of beer caps in different places since then but when I have, I rarely remembered those beer caps. I have seen caps and been reminded of neighbors playing a game with bottle caps as a kid. I remember a time I was at an event and finding a cap that had been completely flattened by a car and I picked it up and threw it like a ninja throwing a star. I even said "I'm a ninja!"

None of those events reminded me at the time of those beer bottle caps from the box. But now as I write this I recalled the memory of those caps to use as an illustration. In certain situations, as needed, I will draw on things of my past in a positive way. My memories do not own me, I own them.

I must also say this. As time has gone by I have realized more and more, two important things. First, and foremost, is that I was not capable of cleaning out and processing my box or my past on my own. It took Jesus to rescue me and clean me up and took some caring Godly people helping me to get through it. But no one could do the work for me. I would have loved to have avoided the responsibility and choices involved in cleaning out the box by asking Pam to do it for me but that never would have worked. She couldn't make those decisions and it wasn't her responsibility.

The second thing is that there are still and always will be, everyday, things being put in my box. I have grown to trust God to keep it safe from ruin, but I have a responsibility to be aware of what is going in it. I don't always have a choice in what gets thrown in my life but I certainly have the choice to decide how it's stored. And if something goes in there that scares me or causes discomfort to take it out and look at, I better take it to God and deal with it immediately.

The Race

Chapter 7

It was while we were attending the basement meetings and after we had become a church, that I gave my first message. I was certain by that point that I was called to be a "preacher," as I called it then, but had little idea what that meant.

I really enjoyed telling people about the things God had done in my life and how learning things from the Bible could help us live a better life. I felt compelled to tell people about how much God loves us and who He is.

God was using so many events from my past to show me how to apply lessons from the Bible in my life. I was unable to relate to the people and ideas in the beginning, but the more I read, the more I was able to see and understand that it is still relevant.

This was the case one day as I read the passage in first Corinthians chapter 9 starting at verse 24. God began to impress on me the life lessons contained in this simple passage and I knew I had to share them. This is the basic story of how I was inspired to give my first message.

"*Do you not know that those who run in a race all*

run, but one receives the prize? Run in such a way that you obtain it. And everyone who competes for the prize is temperate in all things."

It goes on to give the motivation for running the race and then finishes with: "But I discipline my body and bring it into subjection, lest, when I have preached to others, I myself should be disqualified."

The word temperate in this case means self-discipline.

I was contemplating the idea of running the race of life with self-discipline after I read it and I quickly was taken back to my time in high school.

When I was in high school I ran with the cross-country team. It seems very strange to me because I was not a sports person but I did enjoy being out jogging in nature. Looking back though, it's very possible I only ran cross country for God to teach me this lesson.

Halfway through the season, as the practice was ending one day, my coach took me aside. This was the only time I remember a one-on-one conversation with him. It did not last long, but a phrase that he used has stuck with me my whole life. He said, "Bob, you could be a very good runner if you trained harder. You run on guts, not training." He tried to explain some things to me, but I didn't care to understand at that time.

It is hard to explain but I just didn't have the mindset to run as if I could win. I ran because I enjoyed the excitement of the race. I thought it would be great to win but never really thought I had the ability to be faster than everybody else. The idea of competing against myself was such a new idea to me I don't think I understood it. I just ran.

No matter the reason at the time, I just couldn't receive in my heart what he was saying.

This passage in the Bible took me back to that day with my coach. That self-discipline is running on training not on guts.

Before I go on, let me tell you what I believe led up to the conversation with my coach.

We were running in a meet against several other schools. For those who don't know, cross-country running in this case, involved runners being sent out at timed intervals to run just over 2 miles through a course marked out through woods, fields, around buildings, or other landscapes. There would be over 150 runners that day sent out in groups. Your start time was noted by your number and then your finish time was noted to figure exactly how long it took you to run the race. Your time was then posted and whoever had the best time won.

If you went out in a middle slot you could finish behind people that ran slower than you. It didn't even mean if you finish first you were necessarily the winner. You could not compare yourself to the person next to you. You had to run your own race.

Not many of our meets were run this way. We usually started all at once but this time there was going to be a big crowd. Also at this particular race, my mom was coming to watch. I was nervous because I wanted to do well in front of her.

It would prove to be a challenge, though. I had left home that morning without my race shoes which were much lighter and made specifically for racing. The tennis shoes I had worn were for looks not running. They were much heavier than race shoes. I tried to get word to my mom to bring my racing shoes with her but had no success.

So there I was, I had the wrong equipment, in a race style I was not familiar with, in a large group of experienced runners, combined with the fact that I was extremely nervous with my mom watching for the first time.

I received my number, my slot and the whistle blew—I was running.

Everything I had been taught seemed to have left me. I started way too fast, not paying attention to my natural starting pace I set out to lead my group. My mind played tricks on me as I watched the stream of runners and the groups in front of me stretched out ahead before they disappeared into the woods where the trail turned.

I was warned that there was some rocky terrain and hills as you came back towards the finish but I was not thinking about that at the start.

Halfway through the race my legs were screaming with pain. By the mile and a half point my breathing was no longer controlled, in through the nose out through the mouth. I was gasping for breath and my chest felt like I had an elephant on it.

Then I turned an uphill corner into the clearing where the finish was. There was gravel and I was spent.

I lost my footing but didn't go down. But the act of catching my balance stalled me, I stopped.

I was sure there was no way I could go on. I would just walk in. Then I remembered my mom being there. I could hear the others in the distance as the earlier runners crossed the line. So I began to run again. Not on my training, not on what I had been taught, not with elegant form or composure. I ran on my guts, on the sheer determination that I would not finish this race walking, giving up.

I finished midfield out of all the runners. Not bad considering I almost quit. Not long after that is when the coach had this talk with me.

It was embarrassing. I never talked about the race with my mom. That was the only meet she went to. I felt so foolish in front of the coach. As he talked I just couldn't receive what he said. I know he was trying to be encouraging but I had lost heart. I finished the season but never raced after that year.

It seems depressing but it's really not. I've learned so much from that time.

One of the many big lessons of that day was where my focus was. I let my focus on the other runners cause me to ignore what I knew I should do. I also ignored what was my natural pace.

In my life, I get myself in so much trouble when I focus on what other people have or their place in life. If I'm not careful, I will get into a mode of reacting to the people and situations of life rather than living life with purpose.

Just like I had a natural starting pace I also have a natural contentment in life. I run to win the prize, but I don't want to burn myself out before I get to the end. If I focus on keeping up with others, I won't be able to run my race and I will either get burnt out or start to slow and not get where I need to be. There is a pace that is just right; not complacent but content.

Recovery is that way too. I remember in the beginning I wanted to hurry up and do what I needed to do so I would be fixed. Trying to sprint through the marathon of the healing God was doing in my life.

I will never be the fastest person in a foot race. I will not win every race of life I run. What the key in life is for me, is to compete against myself in all I do. I must strive to do better each day. Being the best is not as important as being *my* best.

Another aspect was conditioning. I had put in a lot of miles of running prior to that race but I was just basically jogging. I was also smoking during that time. The jogging was just going through the motions of training. I should have been disciplining my body to prepare it for race conditions. Not just jogging down the road. The whole being temperate or self-disciplined in all things aspect of that scripture in order to run to win the prize.

That is also how I have to live life. I have to live each day with a purpose and meaning. Not just going through the motions but making each choice count. For instance, if I'm going to spend time with family I need to put down my phone and really spend time with them.

When it's time to work I'll give 100% and not 75% with the idea of making it up later. When it's time to relax and unwind or have fun I don't let work or ministry occupy my mind and distract me. I focus on the moment and let God take care of everything else.

In running, the more intense miles you put in, the easier it is to go the distance later. It's that way with making good choices in life. When we talk to God and choose to do the right thing, the easier it is to keep talking to God and keep choosing to do the right thing.

Another is the need to have the right equipment. I had tennis shoes that day but what I needed was running shoes. In the book of Ephesians chapter 6, there are many pieces of equipment described for us to use in the battles of life. I've seen people describe going through the motions of pretending to put these things on. There is a difference between having or wearing the equipment and actually knowing how to use the equipment on race day or in battle. These things are only of value when you know their *purpose* and how to *use* them. *We must also train with these things and not just wear them.* We can't go through life dressed like we're going to the Renaissance Fair rather than being equipped for battle.

Finally, I can't stress the lesson enough I learned about listening to my various coaches. Our coach may be a pastor, spiritual leader, recovery sponsor or mentor. Coaches can see things in our training and competing that we can't see when we are in the middle of it. Good coaches can encourage us to reach new levels that alone we could never reach. They can help us implement new techniques for handling life's situations that will help us to overcome.

The ultimate coach though is the Spirit of God who

dwells in us. Having a relationship with Him will save your life on many levels. Listening to Him on a daily basis is always better than Him pulling us aside later to correct us.

Remember, if you don't run to receive a prize, you're not racing, you're exercising. Run for the prize!

Soaring With The Eagles
Chapter 8

Early in my walk with God the church we attended would sometimes, as a group, attend services at another church where worship could last for several hours and the congregation often ministered to each other during that time. God had brought me a long way in that I was not just enduring the worship music until we got to the teaching.

I would escape into my mind where it was just me and God and I would sing to Him and at times He would speak to me about things through the music. Much of the time, this involved Him teaching me how He felt about me, about who I was and who He wanted me to be.

During one particular service, the music had been going on for 30 to 45 minutes. We had gone on an emotional journey up and down, waging spiritual warfare and resting in His peace. As often was the case, there were times when a period of spontaneous worship would come and these times would involve repetition of a phrase, usually from a principal in the Bible.

During this particular worship time the phrase was

"I will soar like an eagle, I will soar like an eagle. I will soar like an eagle in Him."

Soon people were stretching out their arms to the side and swaying with the music as if they were soaring above it all. I, however, was kind of ready to move on with the service. I was a little tired and ready to sit down.

I watched as I sat there in that room with 30 or 40 people, the majority of whom were soaring. The music had an excitement about it with an almost reassuring feel. It was not fast, not slow, not loud, but not soft. And this is when I began a conversation with myself, inside my head of course.

It went along the lines of how goofy these people looked. Many of them were actually like little kids. Some of them were laughing, some were crying and some just looked peaceful. I didn't get it, what's the big deal? You're soaring. Let's move on.

But then another idea came in. "What's wrong with them having fun or expressing the way they feel?"

This had to be God joining the conversation because I was not going that direction. I thought, in answer to that idea, they look silly and God wouldn't want people acting like that in church.

"How do you know what God would want," I thought?

"And isn't that exactly what King David did as his wife sat back and judged him? Didn't he look silly to her? And he didn't care what people thought."

"Well that's different," I thought.

"Why?" The idea came.

And so went the conversation in my head for a minute or two. I can't remember all the words but what God was making me see was that I cared way too much what people thought of me. And I was way too quick to judge other people's relationship with God based on what I saw on the outside.

I actually began thinking I wished I could just let go sometimes and be free to do what I wanted to do. That was why I liked drinking. I didn't care what people thought. I just did whatever came to my mind to do. Obviously, because I was drunk, terrible ideas were plenty and my ability to get control was gone so it rarely went well.

So there I was, having this crazy, in depth conversation in my head while all these people are soaring like eagles.

And then came the thought; "Well, why don't you just get up and do it?" So I got up.

"But I can't just start pretending like I'm soaring, I'll feel stupid".

"That's the whole point of this, so why would you feel stupid?",

"I'll feel stupid because I'll look awkward and silly."

"That's what you think other people think. But you have no idea what they will actually think. You're feeling made up feelings."

"No, I'm pretty sure I'll look awkward because that's the way I feel and that's real."

"So what if they do think that? Are you going to spend the rest of your life missing out because of what people think?"

That was it! Suddenly, as if my whole life flashed through my mind, I saw that I had spent most of my life missing out on things I wanted to do because of what people might think of me. I did so many things I didn't want to do because I worried about what people thought of me. So much of who I had become was shaped by what other people's opinions might be.

"That's it, I'm doing it. I don't care what anybody thinks!"

And the music stopped...

It was over and I missed my chance once again to try something new. How unfair is this? I go through all of this stuff in my head and just when I decide I'm going for it, it's over.

"So go up and asked them to do it again so you can soar."

"What!"

"Go ask them to do it again and tell them why."

"I can't do that, there is no way I'm going to do that."

"Isn't that the whole point? You're tired of missing out on life because of what people think. This is the perfect chance to do something different."

And so I did. I suddenly felt like none of the stupid stuff mattered. Yes, I was scared and a little embarrassed, and I did think they might say sorry it's time to move forward with the service. There was the real chance that I was completely out of order and it was improper for me to do this. But desperate men do desperate deeds.

A lifetime of missing out on things, hiding who I really was and pretending to be someone I'm not made me a desperate man.

I found myself walking up the aisle to the pastor of the church and asking, "Can we do that again?" "I want to soar and I was too embarrassed to do it then. I don't want to miss out on what God has for me because of what people might think."

"Of course we'll do it again, but first tell everybody what you just told me". And there was suddenly a microphone in my face. So I did, and we did it again. And I soared like an eagle! And so did everyone else. No one judged me, they were happy that I overcame.

God has used that moment more times than I can remember to help me step out in hard times. Most of the time things work out great. Sometimes though it does not, sometimes it goes the opposite of the way I think it should, that's life.

Sometimes we step out and fail. Sometimes people make fun of us or judge us critically. I have the choice to move on and shake it off or stay stuck in the prison of people's opinions. I still want to live my life to the fullest, walking in what God has for me regardless of what people might think.

Getting My Voice Back

Chapter 9

Not long after I learned to soar like an eagle I had begun to play the guitar. I had written some songs and had led worship at times in the little church. That in itself was a miracle in my life. Standing in front of people singing and playing guitar was something I would never had been able to do apart from God.

Worship had actually become an incredibly important part of my life. I am not a talented singer but my heart still soars with God when I sing. God used worship music to minister to me and taught me intimacy with him through it.

Time moved on and so did Pam and I. God moved us out of that little storefront church and we began attending a much larger church across town. It was very hard to leave the little church; we had made so many very close friends there and had built our lives around being part of that ministry. We had been part of that community for several years but it was time to go. Pam and I both were broken-hearted about it.

My work was changing as well. I was now involved

in sales and management of remodeling projects. This gave me a little more freedom in my schedule and a little more money. But the owner of the company was tied, in a way, to the little church so I began to wonder about my security there in the long run.

My voice had become more important in my life between work and in my relationship with God. I was talking with people all the time and there were times when my voice would seem to just give out.

I would rest it for a while and it would come back so I didn't think much about it in the beginning. After a while though, I would lose my voice and barely be able to speak above a whisper for days at a time. After a year or so of this I began to get a little worried and would talk to God about healing whatever may be going on in my throat.

Financially we were just starting to recover from the years of bad choices and unfortunate circumstances. While this was good, we were still not able to afford health insurance yet. People would ask if I had been to the doctor and I would just tell them it was nothing, it probably just had to do with some neck issues I had and it would get better soon.

I was actually getting a little worried and would more and more often find myself not just asking God to heal my voice but telling Him, "You have to do something." Not a good place to be.

I was afraid to go to the doctor for a lot of reasons. Partly I was in denial about what the real problem could be. My grandfather had years of surgeries and not being able to talk from smoking. I was afraid of what that would mean. I had quit smoking several years earlier, but I thought maybe my bad choices in the past may have come around to take their revenge.

In the end though it mainly came down to what it would mean for us financially. Doctors and hospitals cost big money and I didn't have any. So I continued to plead with God to do something.

Another six months went by. The episodes of losing my voice came more frequently and would last longer. Singing more than a minute or two was a huge task and conversations with clients were now becoming exhausting.

After talking for twenty minutes, I would feel like I had run five miles. It took so much concentration and effort to just form words loud enough to be understood. And now it wasn't just wearing me out. Things were happening inside of me that I couldn't see. As a result of not being able to sing I had stopped playing the guitar. This had the side effect of causing me to avoid worship times with God. The more time passed and the more I needed him the less time I spent with him.

One of the side effects of my voice being very hoarse and weak sounding was the way I approached conversations. People I knew had stopped saying anything about it, but it seemed they were getting frustrated trying to talk with me about anything in depth. It took me a lot longer just to say simple things during those times. Speaking in front of groups of people was almost impossible.

The list of things coming against us was growing out of control. The loss of our old church family and things that were connected to that, the difficulties that situation caused with my work and now the challenges caused by my voice giving out were starting to weigh me down.

I was beginning to wonder if maybe I had done something to mess everything up that I didn't know about. And if I hadn't done something to make God mad, why was He allowing this stuff to happen? This is never a good place to be.

The new church we were attending had started announcing worship team tryouts. They were taking place the following month. I thought maybe that would be a good way to get connected in the new church, but I was very nervous about even hoping it could happen.

My confidence was so low and my trust in God had gotten very shaky. I felt like I had been having faith that He would take care of me but with everything going on I just wasn't sure He was listening.

For the previous few weeks, my voice had been getting better but it was still very raspy and sounded like I had a bad cold. Then for no apparent reason, it was gone. No matter how hard I tried I could barely speak above a whisper. After a week and a half, it was time. I had to go to the doctor; I couldn't rationalize or deny it any longer. Something was wrong.

I didn't even have a doctor; I scheduled an appointment with my dad's doctor and he referred me to a specialist. He looked at my vocal cords through a scope and said I had a long growth that was folding over between my vocal cords preventing them from closing properly. I would have to have surgery to have it removed and then they would do a biopsy to see if it was cancer. He said it was best to do it right away. I said I needed a week to get things ready at work for me to be gone. I was scheduled for surgery on Halloween.

Something happened…I don't know what exactly or why, but scheduling that surgery gave me a shove. A few days later I went to the worship pastor of the church and explained that I was scheduled for throat surgery in a couple of days and couldn't be at tryouts. I explained that I would like to try out ahead of time if possible. He said I could bring my guitar after the next service and could try out then. My hope was to be able to play acoustic guitar in the back of everything.

My oldest daughter who was in her early teens stayed with me. I played and managed to sing a song for him that I had written years earlier. I was only able to sing a verse and chorus, but that was enough. He said it was great and compared the sound of my voice to Joe Cocker's. It seemed like a compliment. I had a place on the team once I recovered.

I was still concerned about where the money for the surgery would come from, but it wasn't like I had a choice. It had to be done and we would have to take each step one day at a time.

My surgery day came and everything went well. I was told it was important that I not talk for a week and they would call me with my biopsy results in a few days.

It was very hard not to talk for a week. There was a time after three or four days that my family and I were sitting around hanging out and somebody said something that struck a funny memory and I spoke out without thinking. It was just a sentence, but everybody stopped because it was like I yelled it. I had to strain so hard, for so long, just to talk in a normal voice that it had become natural to me and I automatically used that same effort this time and it boomed out.

A couple days later we got the biopsy results back, no cancer. For some reason though, it didn't even register in my mind that there would be cancer.

From that first doctor's visit to my surgery, it had taken eight days, then another seven days recovery. After almost a year and a half of dealing with this, I physically got my voice back in fifteen days.

In the weeks and months that followed I would think back about everything that went through my mind leading up to my going to the doctor. I couldn't believe that I put it off for so long; it made me feel kind of stupid.

I can't say exactly how the answers to all this fell into place, I just know at a point down the road I understood a lot about myself because of this situation.

Faith, I began to understand, was something that was taught as a force that is within us as believers. I had bought into the idea that if you believe for something hard enough without doubting you would be rewarded with that thing you believed for. I did not consciously think, "Okay Bob, believe and you shall receive". It was more along the lines of, I asked God to heal me and He knows I don't have any money so why wouldn't He just heal me. And when it didn't happen I figured it must be because I was doing something wrong or, I was somehow doubting.

Forms of this idea of faith were very common at that time on television and in many churches so it is understandable how I came to believe it.

In time, God used this circumstance to teach me that I had it completely wrong about faith. As I studied the Bible on my own I began to see that faith is not a power within us like "The Force" from Star Wars that we can wield to accomplish our every wish. Faith is trusting that God has the power to accomplish whatever needs to be done to bring about His will. But that does not mean the He is maleficent (harmful or evil in intent or effect). Neither is He Santa Clause or a Genie in a bottle, granting wishes and gifts as we see fit. Combined with this belief in His absolute power is the understanding that He has my best interest in the forefront of whatever He does in my life. Understanding that I can trust Him with my life no matter what it looks like, and in fact, quite often in spite of what it looks like.

God showed me that I was trying to force my will on that situation because of my perspective of what I felt I needed. I had no insurance and very little money and it had been that way for a very long time. Living from that perspective caused me not to see His provision in the right way.

I walked in fear of not having enough and the way that made me feel. Those feelings of not being able to pay my bills and missing out on things ruled many of my decisions. When I live that way it causes me to make emotional decisions based on my wallet instead of wisdom and God's leading.

As time passed God showed me that not only could

He take care of me physically by giving me my voice back but He also could work things out to provide for me financially. He didn't do this in the same way He did our other medical bills when Pam had our second baby. In this case I set up a payment plan and God provided extra work and opportunities to save money so we could pay off the debt completely.

It has not been uncommon for me to have to learn the same lesson from many different angles before I start understanding how things work. God's patience in teaching me that I can trust Him with my life always amazes me.

Aside from the money issue, even more important in my life, is the peace of being able to trust God. Pam and I started our family so young and made so many bad choices in the beginning, it started us out at a definite disadvantage. When things start that way it becomes normal for them to *be* that way.

When I was living without hope for my financial future, feeling like I would always be behind, I made emotional choices without regard to the real consequences for the future. Having trust that God is watching out for me and will provide for us gives me that hope and peace for the future.

Taking it one step further, the trust that God has earned in my life causes me to see that I can trust Him in every area of my life, not just financially. Actually, God cares more about my work, relationships, ministry and day to day life than anybody I know.

There is another voice I had to learn about, my inner voice. The voice I talk to myself with on the inside.

This voice is every bit as important as my physical voice.

    I did not know it at the time, but my inner voice was coming and going as well. And, in my times of weakness I was at the mercy of the *"other"* voices in my head.

Sometimes You Have To Honk For Yourself

Chapter 10

Not long after my throat surgery I got the opportunity to set out on my own in the remodeling business. I had been working as an independent contractor for the company I was with. I would sell and manage the jobs from leads they provided.

After a year of focusing on the administrative side of the job with the remodeling company I was working for I realized I enjoyed being part of the actual production. The owner and I worked out a pay and bonus schedule to allow me to get my hands dirty.

He went for it and while it provided me great experience, after a couple years I could see that if I was going to grow any further I would have to be on my own. I began asking God to make a way for that to happen and a few months later He did. It was exciting and scary and incredibly hard work.

I accepted any work that came along; siding, kitchens, room additions or garages—anything I could make money at and fit into my schedule. It is actually more profitable to specialize but I loved the variety and it made it easier to keep myself busy.

I hired helpers as needed, but it was pretty hard to find reliable help that fit into that situation. I would basically have to train them for each job and we might not do the same type of job for another six months.

It took a lot to make my business a success. I would sell the jobs; I ran materials, did the work myself and did my best to keep up with the paperwork. Pam helped with the paperwork for taxes and other things when time permitted, it was pretty hard keeping it going.

During that same time period we left the church we were attending. I didn't want to but the leadership kept doing things that were very manipulative. Everyone from the senior pastor, youth pastor, worship leaders, mission's director and children's pastor were all members of the same family. Parents, grandparents, siblings and children filled all the leadership positions and were on the payroll. Big money decisions were being made by the leadership and from my perspective no one had a voice in that outside of the leadership.

Finding a new church is not as easy as just attending the next one in order down the street . We were kind of wandering about in search of a church family.

I really felt like I had the weight of the world on my shoulders. I was getting tired on the inside and didn't realize it. The long hours and feeling alone had brought me to the point of burnout. I still talked to God and had my times of communion with Him but the tone of our conversations had changed.

In my weakened state, bitterness and resentment began to creep in. I was starting to really feel sorry for myself. A lot of my thoughts started with "if only".

One morning on my way to a job I was having one of these episodes. I was complaining to God about all the stuff that had happened and everything I had to do.

Whenever I tell this story it makes me feel kind of silly. I knew what the Bible said about forgiveness and I knew deep inside that God would take care of me but when you're in the middle of a battle sometimes it's hard to look at things in the right perspective. Sometimes when we get weakened by situations or events in our lives it can be really hard to see the things that God is doing. And when we're alone spiritually, it can be very hard to overcome.

That morning in my truck as I drove to the job I was trying to sort through everything but it just made me tired and I felt alone even though I knew God was there.

I usually would have the radio on listening to the Christian radio station in our area. It had nationally known preachers and teachers on each day and I have learned so much from them over the years. That morning I did not feel like listening, I just wanted quiet.

My window was down and it was a beautiful spring morning. The sun was just starting to come up so it wasn't dark but it wasn't fully daylight yet. I don't think I was actually talking to God at that point; I was just feeling lonely and tired and wishing God would do something.

The route I took to this job had me cross over a large storm water run off stream in a mostly residential part of town. A majority of storm sewers in that part of St. Louis empty into this run off called River Des Peres. There is a mix of old broken concrete and rocks that line the run off to prevent erosion and it has pools of water here and there. It empties into the Mississippi not far from where I was at. The bridge over it is about twenty car lengths long and there are traffic lights at each end. I was stopped waiting for the light in about the middle of the bridge.

This bridge doesn't really feel like a bridge because the level of the road stays flat, there is no rise or fall on the approaches. There are four traffic lanes, a center turn lane and side walks on each side but no upper structure, just short guard rail walls.

Everything felt so quiet, actually peaceful. It was still early and there wasn't much traffic out yet. As I sat waiting for the light I began to hear the faint sound of a goose honking. It quickly grew louder and louder and I turned my head to look out the driver's side window. There was a goose flying towards me following the run off. I watched as it came honking for all it was worth and flew right over the hood of my truck. It was windshield level as it passed and continued down the run off, its honk growing faint just as quickly as it had started.

It was like time slowed as this happened and I saw it in slow motion. It also felt like every other sound and movement around me stopped, it was just me and this goose.

All of this happened in the span of the traffic signals changing but it seemed to have lasted for ten minutes. Then, the signal changed to green and the cars in front of me went and I followed in a strange fog of wonder.

About the time I got through the intersection my mind went back to a story I had heard at least ten years before. I had been at some kind of team building seminar and the speaker was trying to get the point across about being supportive.

He said the reason geese fly in a "V" formation is because it is more aerodynamic. The lead goose however, has to take the heaviest load so it is believed that all the geese behind are honking to motivate the leader. After a time, when the leader gets tired, it will fall back in formation and a new leader will take over.

This poor goose had no one behind it to honk for it.

Suddenly on the inside I hear the words... "Bob, sometimes you have to honk for yourself."

I pulled up to the job a minute or two later and just sat there and repeated to myself. "Bob, sometimes you have to honk for yourself."

I knew this had to be God; there is no way that was just a coincidence. A lone honking goose flies over my truck at that exact moment, so close I could have touched it. My window down, the radio off and I was needing encouragement so bad. And then the goose story from years before suddenly comes back to me.

I had chills, I could feel it. God had orchestrated all those events to speak to me in a way I could understand.

For days I thought about what all that meant. In that time what was overwhelming to me, even after all I had been through, was that the creator of the universe was again there communicating with me, talking to me. No matter how I felt, I was never alone.

What I learned from that in the weeks ahead was that I need to encourage myself during those times and stop looking for affirmation from the outside. It does feel good to have someone tell me that I can make it through a difficult situation, but I can't rely on that.

Even now, if you're around me during stressful situations you'll hear me say out loud, "You got this Bob" or something close to it. When I encourage myself out loud I seem to listen better. At times I have to be stern and say; "Come on Bob, you're slacking off!"

Sometimes I find myself in situations where talking to myself out loud could be a problem. In those cases, I'll actually clap which I know seems weird. But it works for me. Try it the next time your in a situation you're struggling in. Just clap at a volume that is appropriate and think to yourself, "You got this, you can do it". It works and nobody will think you're crazy, maybe a little strange but not crazy.

The long term lesson I learned from this is that I have an inner voice. And just like my natural voice, I can lose it.

I had learned that the Bible says we are to take every thought captive, imaginations and pretenses that go against what we know to be true. The problem was I didn't know how to apply that to my life. I've since learned that I have to replace thoughts with other thoughts. Positive thoughts, uplifting thoughts.

During that time in my life there were all kinds of voices in my head speaking to me. Saying things like, "you're not good enough" or "you'll never be successful," and "you're a terrible husband" or "you're a terrible dad," and on and on. The more isolated I became the more those voices convinced me to isolate myself even more.

Sometimes the voices were the words negatively spoken over me by other people replaying in my head. There were voices of darkness that sought to build a wall between me and God. Sometimes it was even my own voice asserting terrible things that had not actually been said but in my mind they must be true. At times these voices tried to convince me I would be better off dead.

I could not just make those voices stop simply by trying to not think those thoughts. I had to tell them to shut up! I had to tell them they have no power over me and they were all lies.

Prior to all this I leaned on people telling me I was good at something or receive other affirmations from outside sources to make me feel better about myself. I would have customers tell me they didn't like something and instead of being able to walk them through the process of fixing it, I would take it personally and lash out at them.

If I made a mistake I would beat myself up for it instead of reminding myself that it's okay to make mistakes; just do your best, learn from it and do better next time. I would often find ways to blame it on somebody or something else just to silence the voices in my head that told me I wasn't good enough.

When I would try to do something to better myself or reach a new goal those voices would tell me not to waste my time because I was never going to change and I would always be a loser.

As a person who had struggled with addiction and messed everything up like I had, it was pretty hard not to believe those voices that tell you, "This is who you are, you're an addict and life is always going to be this way. You're always going to feel this way and there is nothing you can do about it!"

I refused then and refuse today, to live my life listening to those voices.

I never want to drink or do drugs again. I know why I did it and I know there is a voice that would like to get me to do those things again. But that's not my voice. That voice belongs to someone else, someone who would like to make me believe there is nothing that can be done for me, it's just who I am.

But then there is that other voice, the one that told me, "Sometimes you need to honk for yourself." He taught me that I have a voice too, and I don't have to listen to those other voices.

I have come to know His voice more clearly over the years. He has actually been there all along but those other voices kept trying to drown His out. They started when I was little and will probably never give up. I don't care what they say. I have a voice, and…

I have already won!

Forgiveness And A.D.D.

Chapter 11

Staying focused in school was always a real problem for me. In third grade I had to have special reading classes because I just wasn't keeping up. Myself and two or three other kids would go out in the hallway a couple times a week and read with a teacher's assistant. It was handled pretty well by the teachers I guess. I didn't feel defective for it but it was the start of my feeling like I was different than the other kids when it came to school.

Trying to keep my mind on school was like trying to herd cats. It wasn't going to happen without a fight. Homework was torture for me and had it not been for my ability to remember things I heard and read so well I probably would not have graduated. Strangely enough, the test during finals actually saved my grades. But in those classes where homework made up a substantial part of the grade I barely squeaked by.

Each new semester, school would be met with the same new resolution, "This time it will be different." I was going to really try harder and get my homework done and get good grades. Only to finish with,"Bob needs to apply himself" on my report card or "you're smart, if you would only try harder".

I had a teacher in the seventh grade that asked my parents during a meeting if I had been tested for a learning disability and said maybe that would be a good idea. She seemed to sense that something was not right. I don't remember what my parents said but I do remember there was awkwardness and the meeting was soon over. My parents knew I was smart so I was never tested in school. A.D.D. was not widely known about then and I did not have hyperactivity. On the inside I was constantly moving, my brain always in fast-forward. On the outside it just looked like daydreaming.

I did not learn about A.D.D. until I was in my early thirties. I was watching a daytime talk show that had a guest that described growing up and what it was like for him at school, it was my story. I got several books about it and researched everything I could find on the topic. The information was so helpful in learning about treatment and in developing ways to deal with situations that were difficult for me to learn in. Just the knowledge that there wasn't something "wrong" with me, my brain just worked different, was such a relief.

I know this is a controversial topic and that there has probably been an extreme over diagnosis of the condition and over prescribing of the medications that treat it. I believe the medical field has the wrong perspective on the use of meds for treatment of ADD but that is not the point of this story. There is power in knowledge but for me it had come very late so there was a lot of damage done.

Over time the embarrassment turns to shame. The frustration of not being able to accomplish something, when combined with the stress to perform, turns into deep anger. The constant lack of affirmation leads to approval seeking behavior.

We all have a story to tell about growing up. Some of those stories are horrific, some are not too bad. None of them are perfect. ADD and all the things connected to it caused me great pain and overshadowed many years of my life so it was kind of a foundational point of pain for me. As other things happened they would build on top of that foundation that became my life.

Feelings of not being good enough, of being ashamed of who we are, feeling different from everybody else and feeling alone in a crowd happens to so many children, for so many different reasons. Those feelings often cause us to make choices as we grow to protect ourselves from further hurt or cause us to find relief from those feelings in many different ways. Usually those behaviors are just as, if not more, self-destructive as the original situations.

Sometimes these things come in gradual waves that slowly erode away our potential for life and sometimes they come in sudden life shattering events that kill who we are inside. I have had several of both of these in my life.

I have sought relief and understanding for as long as I can remember. I didn't consciously know this most of the time but it is obvious when I look back over my life. I think when people speak of finding the meaning of life they are only kind of speaking of a grand motivation that will give them purpose for the future.

I believe when the majority of people seek out the "meaning of life" they are actually asking, "What's the point of having to endure all the pain and suffering I go through?"

In my process of recovery, which I see as my process of discovering my true self and purpose in life; I have had to get deep down honest with myself. I wore a mask and pretended to be someone I was not for so long that I had no idea who the me inside really was. I bought into the lie that I could make myself into the person I wanted to be if I would just try harder so I formulated a person that I thought would make me happy.

It may be true that we can develop characteristics that seem beneficial to reaching our goals, but unless they are rooted in who we are, they will be incredibly difficult to maintain.

When my past and who I had been, the things I had done and that had been done to me caused me to fall short I was forced to a point of action. It was either my fault I was not where I felt I should be in life or something or somebody else's. I did what so many others naturally do. I sought to find the situations or more specifically the people I could blame for the terrible injustice of my life.

I did not consciously do this. It happens like jerking your hand away from an open flame or a man desperately grabbing for anything when he is drowning. It just happens.

This has been the number one barrier to my growth in life—Blame. It is called by many other names, bitterness, resentments and unforgiveness.

Holding on to these things kept me from taking responsibility for how the rest of my life could be. Maybe all the painful things that had happened to me were terrible and a reason for anger and hurt. But there was a point where I had to understand that today could be the first day of the rest of my life. What happened yesterday can't be undone but today can be the first day of a completely new life.

God gave me tools through a recovery program to help me deal with my unforgiveness. The first person I needed to learn to forgive was myself. God walked me through a process with the help of some great people to understand that I had learned coping skills and was in survival mode and this caused me to make some pretty bad choices.

It may not have been my fault I was in that place but I had a responsibility to make things right to the best of my ability and a responsibility to not repeat those same bad choices.

I learned that hurting people hurt people. I also discovered that broken people break people and needy people take from people. I had been all three of these things, hurt, broken and needy. I had hurt people, broke people and taken from people because that was what had happened to me; and that was what had happened to the people that had done it to me. A cycle that would continue until someone said enough, "It stops with me".

There is no way to explain how this understanding happened apart from God's love. It gave me value and worth and helped me see that I was important to Him, regardless of how anybody else felt about me.

Beginning to forgive myself allowed me to begin to forgive others. I slowly began to understand that the majority of things that had happened to bring me pain in my life were not directed at me personally. I was generally a victim of circumstance and people's reactions to their own hurt, brokenness and need. It was not my fault but in most cases it wasn't their fault either. And in the cases where it was their fault or choice, I had a choice in what I would do with the results of it.

I could live stuck in the past, a continual victim of their actions and my choice. Or I could let today be the first day of the rest of my life and leave them behind to deal with it between them and God.

Neither of these happened right away or easily. In some situations I still have times today where I have to consciously remind myself of what I learned twenty years ago. Forgiveness is hard but involves every aspect of our lives in some way so it is critical to our moving forward.

Finally, I had to forgive God. I couldn't have even said that out loud in the beginning. It seemed so wrong to me from what I had been taught. When I did start to talk about it with others I had a few people get offended that I would even think that I had something I needed to forgive God for or the ability or authority to do it.

God after all was perfect. How could we as imperfect humans think we could forgive God?

But I did need to forgive Him. I was hurt and mad

that He let the things that happened to me happen. If He was all powerful then He could have stopped it. So He either didn't care about me or He was punishing me for something I didn't deserve.

I was also told that I was fearfully and wonderfully made. So why did I have ADD? But He taught me that the label of Attention Deficit Disorder was a humans' explanation for a gifting they didn't understand.

God had given me unique talents and giftings that would be necessary for the calling He had placed on my life. Mankind had structured society in ways that did not allow for my particular giftings. They had to do this to accommodate the education of the largest amount of people possible. My inability to thrive in that environment was met and dealt with through the understanding of everyone involved in the best way they knew how. And through it all He was able, once I surrendered my hurt and resentment, to bring me to the place He wants me to be.

In my immaturity in the beginning I was afraid to speak out about forgiving God because of people's ignorance of who God is. After a while I would talk with certain people in safe situations because of fear of offending someone.

Now I understand that the majority of people who I meet that reject God is not because they haven't heard about Him. It's because they don't understand who He is and they hold some type of bitterness towards Him.

It seems crazy that God would be willing to accept responsibility for all of our flaws and dysfunctions, our willful disobedience and rebellion and let us "forgive" Him for stuff He is not responsible for. But that is exactly what He has done because He loves us that much.

Even crazier is that He has given us the ability to forgive Him and without that ability when left to our own strength and understanding we would never choose to seek Him. But He loves us so much that He is willing to forgive us for our mess so we can find forgiveness for ourselves and others, including Him.

And there is freedom in forgiveness, the only true freedom there is. Freedom cannot exist apart from forgiveness.

We often hold on to unforgiveness and hurt because of what has been done to us. To let go of that hurt often feels like we are letting people off the hook for the wrongs they have done. Especially when it comes to abuse of any kind, letting go and forgiving the perpetrator seems like a free pass for their behavior.

Sadly though, we cannot compartmentalize unforgiveness or resentments. They always run below the surface no matter how hard we try to control them. Even when we have long stretches of success with holding the hurt in, eventually something will trigger it and the beast is released; sometimes through lashing out at others, sometimes in harming ourselves.

The situations and issues that cause us the resentments, bitterness or unforgiveness must be dealt with to find true freedom. Dealing with them is almost impossible on our own.

That is what this book has been about, Freedom.

I was in a prison of my own and other peoples design. I thought I had a life sentence of addiction, depression, failure, hopelessness, shame, self-destruction, guilt, deception, hiding, delusion, loneliness and despair.

But I found freedom from all these things. It was the simplest most difficult thing I've ever done. You can start your journey right now too if you want.

Today can be, THE FIRST DAY OF THE REST OF YOUR LIFE

Salvation
When You Need A Do Over

Chapter 12

God had a simple plan to save us from ourselves that we have determined to complicate as humans because that is what we do. There are spiritual forces at work behind the scenes that also create havoc but there is no need to worry about that now. They don't really measure up to the amount of trouble most people think they do.

God had a plan from the beginning for us to have a relationship with Him. Mankind made a choice to separate ourselves from him through a single choice but that choice is played out in every life on earth in every moment of the day.

I described just a few of the events in my life that brought me to a point of complete surrender of myself to God. Maybe you are at the point where you know you have to do something different but don't know what or how.

The basics are that we as individuals cannot be good enough to earn a relationship with God on our own. We will by nature do things that separate us from God. Those things are often referred to as sin. Sins are crimes against God, ourselves or other people. There is no sliding scale or acceptable level of sin or crimes. A sin is a sin, even if it is just a thought we may have that we never intend to act on.

Knowing this, God gave of himself as the price for justice for our wrong doings or crimes. He sent his son to die on the cross as a sacrifice for the penalty of sin. It seems pretty brutal and maybe a little extreme to think about but that is how serious a situation we are in. Over time God will guide you in understanding the deeper details and symbolic biblical ideas for all of this but you don't have to know them to start. He knows exactly what pace is perfect for us and he will make sure we are never behind if we just listen.

It doesn't take a deep theological discussion or idea to just surrender to God. In fact it is as easy as saying, "Jesus, I need you to come into my life and change me and make me new. I give you permission to do what ever it takes to make me whole. I'll do my best to trust you even though I don't really know what this all means right now. Just please help me and make me new. I receive the sacrifice you made in my place".

That's it. Yes it is that easy and that simple to start. Of course there will be times in your journey that you are going to want to quit, to go back to what is normal to you. When you have those times, we all do, you can say this prayer again to reaffirm your decision. The important thing is to run to Him when we struggle even though we may want to run and hide.

It is also important to learn who God is for ourselves. There are a lot of different opinions out there and not all of them are healthy or even true. God gave us the Bible to help us learn who he is and how to live while here on earth and even a little about what it will be like after we die. That way we can be sure because as humans we can tend to twist things to fit what we want at the time.

Sometimes people have a real hard time reading the Bible and applying it to their lives. I know, I was one of them. God guided me to some very good teachers to help me and he helped me surround myself with people who have good healthy relationships with Him. It is a good idea to find a healthy church to be part of as long as attending or serving at that church doesn't take the place of having a relationship with Jesus. It is easy to get caught up with checking off things to do to be a good Christian and forget that being a Christian is about a relationship with Christ and not about what you do at church.

There are some people who can repeat a lot of things from the Bible and seem to be very religious but that doesn't mean they have a relationship with Him. Just watch and you'll see who they are. Don't try to argue with them. God will take care of it.

If going to church right now is too much to start or if you attend church and feel like you need more of a recovery based approach I would encourage you to find a Celebrate Recovery in your area. The tools you will learn from CR can change your life. If the first CR doesn't fit, try another one.

Talk to God about everything. He wants you to, He loves you. Even the stuff that makes you embarrassed or feel ashamed. He wants you to tell Him what you think and how you feel.

As time goes you are going to hear a lot about sin and the bad choices you may make. Don't let that discourage you. You didn't have to earn your forgiveness and you can't be good enough to keep it. You're going to make mistakes and sometimes bad choices. And sometimes you will have to walk in the consequences of those things but remember, God is not punishing you. It just takes walking in the pain of our bad choices for us to learn sometimes.

Sometimes people feel like they have done so much bad that they have to earn God's love. I promise that is not true.

As people, we continually fall back into trying to make ourselves feel better about who we are. Because of this, when we make mistakes or "sin" we tell ourselves we are forgiven, which we are. Sometimes though, we use this to give ourselves permission to keep on doing things we shouldn't. Things that will bring hurt to ourselves or others, maybe not right away, but in time.

The Bible says Jesus paid the price once for all our sins so we no longer have to worry about that. When we face any choices in our lives we should ask ourselves...

"Will this draw me closer to God or push me away?"

If we let this be a guiding principle in our lives we will avoid so much pain and heart ache. Even if we get it wrong to start with we will soon learn that we are drifting from God and seek Him to help us know what it is that is separating us from Him.

My hope and prayer is that you find who you are and realize you are special; that you find Freedom in life,

Hope for the future and Peace in recovery.

Remember you are not alone. God loves you!

CPSIA information can be obtained
at www.ICGtesting.com
Printed in the USA
JSHW011534130819
1081JS00004B/5

What do you do when you realize you have become someo[ne] you would not like to be friends with? What if you realized [the] things you were doing to make you happy were not workin[g?]

When we start out to **change** who we are or what direct[ion] our life is going, it can become very **discouraging.** When [we] are not instantly successful or situations are not sudde[nly] perfect, it is easy to **give up** and slip back into **old routin[es.]**

The great thing is **we don't have to do it alone**, there is he[lp.] Sometimes if we will just pause and look around we see that [help] has been there all along. We just didn't know to look fo[r it.]

Bob has over 30 years of being free from drugs and alcohol. Bob and his wife Pam are co-founders of Real Life Ministries, helping others find freedom, hope and peace through the recovery process. They are currently ministry leaders of a local Celebrate Recovery meeting.

Bob and Pam have been married for over 33 years. They have two happily married daughters and four young grandchildren.

WHAT DOES IT MEAN TO BE "BAPTIZED IN HOLY SPIRIT"?

THE MEANING OF "EATING MY FLESH AND DRINKING MY BLOOD" IN JOHN 6:5-61

THE LORD JESUS CHRIST WASHING THE FEET OF HIS DISCIPLES (JOHN 13:4-17)

THE NON-LITERAL MEANING OF WATER IN THE NEW TESTAMENT SCRIPTURES

FIRST PUBLISHED: 2012

By: A scribe discipled into the kingdom of the heaven